Soul Piercing

John 12:46

Laurie L. Ferris

Cover Art: Ian Grinyer; griny477@aol.com

All Scripture is from the New American Standard version of the
Bible unless otherwise noted.

Dedication

Enoch walked with God; and he was not, for God took him—these words rang out in the village at the gravesite of a wonderfully special young boy named Mailie Justice Mangena.

I'd like to dedicate this book to Mailie, in honor of his boldness for God's Word. Mailie touched many lives even up until his last moments before God took him home. On that appointed Sunday, we had baptized eighty-three people in the river in the village of Moshakga, South Africa. Mailie was on his way home from the baptism when he stopped at another boy's home. A mother was crying. Other mothers were there comforting her. Mailie at the young age of eleven years, asked if he could pray for this mother. Immediately after praying, Mailie walked up the hill to cross the road and was hit by a drunk, unlicensed driver. As I cried out to the Lord we all trusted, He spoke audibly to me, "Mailie loved Me." What greater testimony? Mailie loved his Lord.

A few weeks passed and those very ladies Mailie met on that Sunday of his homecoming came to his father's church (His dad is the Pastor). When his mom, Agnes, asked how they came to know our church, they explained that a young boy came to pray with them. They were told he passed away only moments later.

A special thank you to Pastors Jonas and Agnes for being such wonderful examples of God's love. Their living testimony gave us this young boy, Mailie. I will never forget him. I have such fond, touching memories of his ministry with me speaking with hospitalized children about Jesus. Jonas and Agnes please know that on the day you are all reunited, you will hear the words, "Well done thou good and faithful servants."

Mailie Justice Mangena walked with God; and was not, for God took him.

Acknowledgements

If you have ever had a dream and have had the pleasure of seeing it come to fruition, you realize that many hands have helped in seeing the dream through. I can't name all those who helped along the way in fear I would, no doubt, leave someone out unintentionally. The following are just a few who never wavered in using their gifts to help me:

Jody Zilske, a gifted writer, has coached me in this publishing endeavor every step of the way. She exemplified the heart of Christ by agreeing to help a sister in need without even meeting me first. Not only do I appreciate the editing, formatting, and computer coaching but most of all the fellowship, which usually ended up in laughter. Jody, I thank you from the bottom of my heart for helping me realize my dream. I pray the greatest success on your writing ministry, you have a tremendous gift.

My youngest sister, Annmarie Gianotti, is a dreamer and therefore my greatest cheerleader. She has cheered me on all the way through. Ann, I hope someday all your dreams come true, as well.

A special thank you to Ian Grinyer who is a very blessed artist. He paints God's world in such a beautiful light. He agreed to let me use his painting for my cover. I wanted a piece of art which spoke of the Lord's Word and presence piercing through the darkness and there it was—his painting.

Thank you, family—statewide and globally. Your stories are in these pages, and I am so blessed to share them.

Last but certainly not least, I want to thank Jesus Christ. My story is actually His Story. He is represented in every one of these pages. Without His amazing love, the stories I share would all have had a very different ending. Thank you, Lord that all things work to good. All our stories have good endings when you are the center.

Introduction

"And Simeon blessed them and said to Mary His mother, "Behold, this Child is appointed for the fall and rise of many in Israel, and for a sign to be opposed—and a sword will pierce even your own soul—to the end that thoughts from many hearts may be revealed."
Luke 2:34-35

Soul piercing: an experience in life that is so profound, so defining, that it goes past piercing the heart and reaches down to our very souls. It shakes the very foundation of who we are and what we have believed. One way or another, we have to take action or else our souls will be in a stand still. We will be stuck.

Most of us have had *soul piercing* experiences. Those times rock us to the core. If we have no foundation, we will sink.

In your hand, you hold a book written from a pierced heart. My prayer is for the reader to see that in our darkest moments, God's Word and His Presence pierce through with light. This light of his Word is powerful enough to separate bone from marrow and sharp enough to pierce our souls. Above all else, I pray the reader will know the Savior Jesus Christ in the most intimate way.

Table of Contents

He Hovers Over Me 11

Always Interceding 18

He's Just Too Good 22

Cup of Rejoicing 26

Abba! Father! 30

Thorns 34

Remember Me 38

I Hope You Dance 42

He Calls You Lily 47

Window Shopping 51

Compassionate Father 55

Be On Watch 58

Jesus Lights Our Way 61

I Hold You? 65

The Tale of Two Sisters 70

Running Wild 75

Feeling Stuck 79

Table of Contents Continued

Fashioned Hearts 83

Beggars 88

No Where to Call Home 91

Blessed for Your Sake 96

Two Trees 100

Straight from the Father's Heart 104

Oh, the Gall 108

He Moves in Great Mercy 113

Bottled Tears 118

Bruised Reeds 122

Higher Ground 126

Forsaken? 130

Little Rocks 136

After Words 141

He Hovers Over Me

"The earth was formless and void, and darkness was over the surface of the deep, and the Spirit of God was moving over the surface of the waters." Genesis 1:2

The above verse of Scripture always slays me. It causes me to want to be on my face in worship at the awesomeness of the Lord God. Imagine with me if you will, this vast expanse. There is nothing present we would be familiar with today. It is dark, void, empty, no real life form yet. Can you hear the rushing of the water? I lived on the seas for two years and can just imagine the blackness of the depths of the waters. It's immensely breathtaking.

Scripture states, "And the Spirit of God was moving over the surface of the waters." The NIV states the Lord's Spirit was hovering over the waters. How I wish I could adequately express how this scene is playing out in my heart and mind right now. There wasn't a glimmer of light. Everything was chaos, and the Spirit of the God of the universe was moving over it all. He was orchestrating all His plans for creation. Nothing came to being without His speaking it.

Nothing ever comes to being without the Lord knowing it. No tears fall, no tree grows, no child is conceived, and no person goes to eternity without His foreknowledge. This is a powerful truth. He spoke everything into being. Nothing mankind experiences is hidden from the Father's sight. He never blinks. If He did, the world would collapse back into chaos.

I've always believed the Lord was in control of all things. It's stated in His word. However, that belief had to be tested and in the past few years, it was tested through some very painful experiences.

Test one. My niece, Ella Rose, was born with a rare life threatening blood disorder, and she needed to have a bone marrow transplant. Her sister Sophia, who was seven at the time, agreed to give her bone marrow. Because the bone marrow being a perfect match was miraculous, all seemed to have the Lord's stamp of approval. So, at age fifteen months that little Peanut underwent thirty-two rounds of chemotherapy. It was disturbing to see the effects of the chemo on this little body. It was heart-wrenching to see my sister, Annmarie, and her husband, Rob, go through this trial. But the worst was yet to come. The baby had developed a rare virus, and she was in critical condition three different times.

I never asked the Lord how He could allow this baby to go through such a horrible experience. Rather, I pleaded with Him to keep His promises to us. He promised to bring this child through. While we were preparing for this time, people in churches were praying. One good friend, Maria, saw Jesus standing over the baby with His right hand touching her head. Maria continued to remind me of that vision. My sister, Annmarie, received a similar experience. She prayed when she arrived at the children's hospital, "Lord, what will this all look like in the end?" Right after she prayed, she saw a butterfly. In her darkest hours, my sister held on to that vision of the butterfly, believing, through piercing pain, the Lord would heal her baby. Several surgeries later, after a year in isolation, true to His Word, the Lord came through. Ella Rose is four now and the picture of health. I don't know if any butterfly could match the beauty of this child and what the Lord has done.

Test Two. Our little Peanut was just coming out of her time in isolation still wearing the effects of the chemotherapy and anti-rejection medication. I'd been so much in prayer for this precious child that I had ignored my own health issues. I had felt a lump on my breast and let it go. The thought of another health scare was overwhelming to me. I'd had biopsies for similar lumps through the years, and they were all benign. I pushed it out of my mind for a while, but there was this nagging feeling that somehow this time was different. Finally, I saw a medical team.

After some tests and a biopsy, I was diagnosed with breast cancer. It was believed to be in the earliest stage, and the prognosis after surgery and radiation was believed to be very positive. I was trying to wrap my head around it all. By the time I got myself ready to go through treatment, there was another cancer spot showing positive on an MRI. This could mean that there was either another cancer or the cancer had spread.

The upcoming surgery was nothing compared to the uncertainty which now plagued me. The night before the surgery, I was alone in my apartment with my thoughts. I called a close friend, Sharon, for prayer. As we were praying, we both saw Jesus standing over my hospital bed. He was singing over me! We actually both voiced this at the same time over the phone. The prayer helped, and I felt peace. However, in the wee hours of the morning, I was up fearing the unknown. I had another MRI scheduled just before the surgery to place wires where the lump was. I am claustrophobic and that made me even more anxious. It was overwhelming, and I was in a very dark place.

The morning of the surgery was chaotic. The anxiety medication made me feel worse instead of better. I was shaking from it, and the room was spinning. I actually looked forward to being knocked out for surgery. As I was being wheeled into the OR, I saw the two big doors coming toward me. I remembered the vision my friend and I saw of Jesus singing over me at my bed side. I whispered, "Okay Lord, this is Your cue." The most beautiful voice interrupted my anxious thoughts. As I entered those doors, my good friend David Ossenfort's voice singing, "There is a River" overwhelmed me with peace. The Lord in His tender mercy was lulling His child to sleep through the voice of a trusted friend. At that moment, David's powerful voice was none other than the voice of God singing over me.

I came out of surgery with wonderful news. The cancer spot showing in the second area was a false positive. I had several weeks of radiation and am now a two year survivor.

Our God is so wonderful, isn't He? He keeps every promise He gives us. I don't know where you are at this moment of your journey. Perhaps it seems very dark where you live. There may be a shroud of uncertainty hanging over you. The deep, deep waters of fear desire to drown you. My great hope is that you will remember this truth. When there was utter chaos, emptiness and darkness, the Lord Almighty, the Great Elohim (Creator) spoke light to dispel the darkness. And there was light. He hovered over the great deep. When nothing in life seems certain, He hovers over you and moves on your behalf, just as He did for my niece and me.

Further Along the Way

Can you think back to a time or times when you thought you had great faith until that faith was tested?

What was going on then? Did you fear the chaos you were experiencing would not end? Now try and remember where you experienced breakthrough. How did you finally pass this test of faith?

As you think back to this experience, does it bring back feelings of fear or anxious thoughts? As painful as it is, place yourself in a quiet corner with the Lord. Focus only on Him and His deliverance in this situation. Take deep breaths knowing you are safe with Him and begin to give Him praise.

I have often thought the previous testing of my niece's trauma and deliverance prepared me for the next test. Do you agree?

Can you see a pattern in your own life where you seemed to go through endless battles? When you came out of those battles, did you see a change in yourself? List changes you experienced in the way you handle testing.

How can you minister to someone else going through a trial in light of your experiences?

Father, we all go through trials. Please help us to remember You alone can make sense out of it all. Bring us to a place of trusting You more.

Always Interceding

"In the same way the Spirit also helps our weakness; for we do not know how to pray as we should, but the Spirit Himself intercedes for us with groanings too deep for words; and He who searches the heart knows what the mind of the Spirit is, because He intercedes for the saints according to the will of God." Romans 8:26-27

The Apostle Paul has told us to pray without ceasing. There are many believers who are people of prayer. They spend many hours praying for the lost, praying for the hurting, and praying for the nation and the world. But even these strong people of prayer, at times, are at a loss for words. Because they are people of prayer, they often see things others may not. They have a keen "knowing" or "insight" and if they are not careful, they can be victims of depression. If they don't guard their hearts, the burden of prayer can be overwhelming.

This reminds me of Hannah in the Scriptures. She desired a son and was barren. She would go to the temple and pray. Her head and spirit were both bowed before the Lord. She was so deeply moved and had so much sorrow of heart that the priest looked on and thought she was drunk. What he misinterpreted as he looked on was Hannah's groaning. She was so heavy within that her lips were moving uncontrollably. Deep utterances were bubbling out of her. She was pleading with the Lord and only He understood her heart. Some of us are right there in place of Hannah today. We are sorrowing in our spirits and are at a loss for words in prayer.

What is the answer? We are clearly asked to pray, to intercede. The above Scripture has the answer. "In the same way the Spirit also helps our weaknesses." The term *helps* here is present tense and means *keeps on helping*. Therefore because the Spirit keeps on helping, He is always helping us in our prayer life. All of us being human are frail at times, even those of us who are people of prayer. The Scripture tells us that the Spirit helps us in our weaknesses. The term *weakness* here means we are sometimes physically, emotionally and spiritually weak; therefore, we don't always know how to pray.

Take heart, dear believer and person of prayer. You may be groaning in your spirit with that groaning being too deep for words. Do you realize you are in good company? All of creation is groaning also and waits for the return of the Lord. And as we all wait, the Spirit of the living God is interceding on our behalf with deep groanings that only He knows and understands. He alone knows the heart and mind of man, and even greater than this, He alone knows the heart and mind of the Spirit Who longs to work through us.

You may feel alone as you pray earnestly for loved ones or for the world around you. Take courage believer. The Spirit is closer than beside you. If you are His, He is deep within you interceding on your behalf in ways you will only realize later on. This is our hope in Him.

Further Along the Way

Do you find yourself to be so heavy-burdened that you are at a loss for words? According to the above Scriptures, where will your help come from?

Do you believe the Holy Spirit intercedes on your behalf continually or only at times when you feel His presence? Now consider what the Scripture states in this matter. How does this help your prayer life?

Spend some time now with the Lord, thanking Him for His help in the most pressing concerns. Then be silent and wait for Him to pray on your behalf.

Father, help us to be quiet and trust that Your Holy Spirit is interceding for us continually. Let us not be discouraged but to press forward, knowing You hear our heart's cry.

He's Just Too Good

"The Lord is good to all and his tender mercies are all over his works." Psalm 145:9

I bent down to wash my client's feet. She is a Catholic believer and asked me to share a Bible story with her during each visit. As I was getting ready to apply needed ointment to her feet, I couldn't miss a chance at an illustrative telling of the time Jesus washed His disciples' feet. Due to my client's illness, she often focused on the negative. This spurned her to bring up Judas as he was present at the last supper and about to betray the Master.

I explained how Jesus knew Judas was about to betray Him. He knew who Judas was and knew his character and intentions. Darkness was about to overtake Judas. It had been calling him for some time now. Jesus, knowing full well where that darkness would lead and how it would hurt Him personally, still loved Judas. He still stooped down and washed his feet.

When I reflect on this act toward Judas, I don't imagine Jesus treating him any differently. I imagine Him being just as tender with his feet as with the others' present. Nothing in Scripture points to Jesus treating Judas as an enemy. In my mind's eye, I can see Jesus' expression just as compassionate toward this sinner as He was toward those at the foot of the cross. I hear His heart pleading, *Forgive him, Father, for he knows not what he does.* Believe it or not, that's the heart of the Savior.

This client and I spoke a while about the matchless love of Jesus. That's when my client made this statement, "I know why people don't believe in Jesus. He's just too good." I wanted to laugh at first but then thought she really had a point here. In a world so fallen, so confused and so consumed with selfish ambition, something or someone completely pure and good is hard to believe. Like we often say, "He's just too good to be true." You know what? By natural standards He *is* too good to be true. But Jesus is supernatural; He's not of this world. And at the same time, ironically, He's Truth itself.

He's unlike the new found love who seems too perfect. Once you know the lover more, you begin to see the imperfections. Jesus, on the other hand, is the complete opposite. The more you get to know this lover of your soul, the more amazed you are by His perfection. You begin to see that the more you surrender yourself to Him, the more secure you feel. The more you love Him the more love you get in return. He's really unlike any person in this life. No matter how well-meaning people are none can compare to Him.

My client's sentiment is shared by many. For those who don't know Him, He seems too good to be true. But to us who love Him, He is all good and Truth itself. The Scripture says that He is good to all and His tender mercies are all over His works. I absolutely love that! Remember today as trials may come, His tender mercies are all over you.

Further Along the Way

Have you had an experience where someone you loved deeply hurt you? Were you able to act toward that person with the love of Christ?

We, as believers, sometimes do get hurt by others in our fellowship. How can we best guard our hearts from getting bitter?

Is it ever righteous for believers to treat someone less loving than others because they have hurt us?

Nowhere in Scripture does it state Jesus treated Judas any differently than the disciples. What does this say about Jesus' character?

The Scripture above says, "The Lord is good to all and His tender mercies are all over His works." How did Jesus demonstrate this toward Judas at the Last Supper? How might this look for us as sinners? How might we imitate this to those who are in need of forgiveness?

Father, at times when we doubt Your goodness, help us to remember all Jesus has done. Help us to recount His provision in our lives. Let the saints say, "God is good all the time and all the time, God is good!"

Cup of Rejoicing

"But I say to you, I will not drink of this fruit of the vine from now on until that day when I drink it new with you in My Father's Kingdom." Matthew 26:29

This Scripture has been touching my heart these past several days. I've been thinking of Jesus' last time dining with His disciples. It was during Passover and usually a very festive time. The disciples are reclining with the Master, the One they had followed and loved deeply. They had seen such wonders.

Then the Lord took the cup of wine and explained that it was the cup of the New Covenant. It represented His own blood, which in just a few hours would be shed for them and us. Jesus had to be somber at this point. The disciples must have noticed a difference in His countenance. Jesus' concern is for His disciples at this moment, not Himself. He was about to experience the greatest battle of His life. He would endure such unbelievable torment, and it hasn't been matched since. Oh, many have been persecuted for the faith since. We see them in media, and it tears our hearts in two. However, as horrendous as their suffering is, none compares with what the Messiah endured. Here's why. The Messiah was completely pure and without sin. He would take on *all* the sin ever committed in the history of mankind. No one else can make claim to this intensity of sacrifice because no one else can claim to be without sin.

And yet, knowing full well the agony ahead, He took that cup, representing His bloodshed for you and me, and He stated, "I will not drink of this fruit of the vine from now on until that day when I drink it new with you in My Father's Kingdom." It is such a loving gesture to all of us that the One who called all things into order, the only begotten Son of God, on the day He would be betrayed, the day He would speak of His coming sacrifice, would look forward to the time when He would rejoice with His followers in His Father's Kingdom. He would reserve this festive experience of drinking this wine for us alone. Are you seeing the Lord's unspeakable love for us today? Scripture states, "But for the joy set before Him He endured the cross." You and I are the joy set before the Messiah. He is actually looking forward to the time when we will all be with Him in His Father's Kingdom.

There are so many reading this today who have felt the pain of the rejection of man. Perhaps no one alive hasn't. I sense the Lord wanting you to be sure that there is One Who loves you more than life itself. He gave His very life so that you could come to

Him. He desires to celebrate His life in you and with you. No one on the earth can or is able to love you deeper than this.

Further Along the Way

In His last hours, Jesus was thinking of the disciples as well as us. Can you think of any time He wasn't putting other's first? Do you ever recall in Scripture Jesus seeing to His own needs before the needs of others?

If we are to live as Christ, what does this say about our daily walk?

Jesus was about to experience great, unspeakable agony, yet He didn't look back. Instead, He looked forward to a time of reconciliation. Can you think of times when you had to make decisions on behalf of loved ones which would cause you great suffering? Did you choose the suffering for their better good? When faced with situations which need spiritual maturity, how can the above Scripture and text help you persevere?

Jesus, during His final days on earth, endured horrible rejection. Can you recall times when you suffered rejection as well? When you consider Jesus always thinking of us more than Himself, even to the point of death, how is this a point of healing?

I pray you realize how very much you are valued and loved by the Messiah. Please take time now to thank Him for pressing through the pain for you. Try to imagine the great joy He has for going forward. Meditate on this joy.

Father, help us to remember Christ's willingness to suffer great agony for us. May we give Him glory by being willing to suffer for the sake of others.

Abba! Father!

"And He was saying, "Abba! Father! All things are possible for You; remove this cup from Me; yet not what I will, but what You will." Mark 14:36

Abba! Father! Do you hear the urgency in the voice of Jesus as He speaks loudly with exclamation, "Abba! Father!"? My soul becomes overwhelmed when I consider the reality of Jesus' anguish here. I see Him kneeling on the ground. I see the sweat like blood flowing from His forehead. I hear the gasps for air as He cries out in total abandon and in total anguish. "Abba! Father! All things are possible for You; remove this cup from Me." He begins by speaking the absolute truth—*all* things are possible for the Father. There is no wavering in His thoughts. Then comes His plea, "Remove this cup from Me."

How many have sat beside a beloved child and looked into the eyes of suffering and saw their expression and heard, "Daddy, Mommy, take this away." You would have moved Heaven and Hell to do so.

Yes, we would move Heaven and Hell if it were possible to save those we love from suffering. And, in a real way, that was what the Father was about to do. He literally brought Hell and

Heaven together that day of suffering. All the whipping His Son would endure that night, all the lashes, insults, and torn skin brought the filthiness of Hell upon His flesh.

"Yet not what I will, but what You will"—are there any more powerful words than these? This is obedience in its purest form. Oh, the agony would be fierce and yet, Jesus, the Messiah, knew He was surrendering to the greater good. Not just the greater good but the Greatest Good for all mankind that night.

In a real sense, Heaven and Hell were moved on that night of suffering. Yes, they collided—and Heaven won!

Some take the garden experience of Jesus lightly. They also take the cross itself lightly. It's become a decorative piece of jewelry. And the resurrection? Some never even give this miracle of miracles a thought.

Today, I want to challenge you to remember Jesus and all that happened. Consider this: where would we be if He had not spoken those precious, anguish-ridden words, "Yet not what I will, but what You will." Where would any of us be? Make it personal today. He did.

Jesus did everything during His time on earth to see the desire of His Father come to fruition. That desire is that you and I be reconciled to Him. We are so amazingly blessed.

Further Along the Way

Try to remember times in your life when your plea was as Jesus' to the Father. You were in an excruciating situation, and you knew God could stop all the pain. He didn't. What have you learned from those times?

Did those times when Jesus allowed pain cause you to identify with other's anguish? Could this be one reason why Jesus Himself had to endure all the suffering? How have these experiences caused change in your spiritual life and in your relationships?

"Not My will but Yours." This was the Lord's plea just moments after His cries for mercy. Do you see the heart of Christ here? He knew where that plea of surrender would take Him.

Are you sometimes fearful that if you pray the same there will only be more suffering in your surrender to God's will? Do you believe we are most like Christ when we are willing to suffer, laying down our lives for the sake of others?

Jesus Himself said, "In this world there will be much tribulation (suffering) but take courage, I have overcome the world." In light of what we have discussed here, how does this bring you comfort and strength?

If we are, in fact, most like Christ in our times of suffering, how does that line up with the message preached, "Just believe Jesus and all will turn out well"? Could we be missing something?

Father, thank You for moving Heaven and Hell on my behalf. May the desire of my heart be the desire of the ages—to see lost souls come to know You.

Thorns

"Then to Adam He said, 'Because you have listened to the voice of your wife, and have eaten from the tree about which I commanded you, saying, 'You shall not eat from it; cursed is the ground because of you; in toil you will eat of it all the days of your life. Both thorns and thistles it shall grow for you; and you will eat the plants of the field.'" Gen. 3:17-18

It was such a wonderfully peaceful day in South Africa. Nancy and I were in our coombi (van), and I had my arm hanging out the side. During our rides through safari, I often hung my arm out the van because it was so very hot that even the slightest breeze against my one arm was welcomed. However, sometimes doing so could cause problems like the time my arm was hanging out and there were two magnificent male lions playing together inches away. But on this particular day, it wasn't as dramatic as that. As my arm hung out, Nancy turned the coombi quickly and my arm grazed a thorn bush. Instantly, I felt pain but it soon lessened. We went about our way looking for animals in the bush.

Later that evening, my arm became painful once again and was all red, inflamed and swollen. This continued for a week or so.

Fortunately, for me no infection occurred, but it was a painful experience for sure.

Thorns are not our friends. From almost the beginning of time, they have been a curse to us. Look at the Scripture above. Thorns were promised as a punishment for sin. They would wrap themselves around things and cause all kinds of havoc. I remember a pastor coming to visit us from the states once. He was unaware of the thorn bush growing out of control just outside the coombi as we parked. He opened the vehicle door and walked into thorns and quickly became entangled. We jumped out of the coombi and very carefully had to unwrap his body. He was hurting for some time afterwards.

If we study the Scriptures, we realize thorns symbolize consequences to sin. Isn't it fitting that we can easily get entangled in our sins, just as my pastor friend got tangled in the thorn bush? We sin, and like brushing up against thorns, we sometimes do not see or feel the full force of it until later on. If we are not careful, sin can be infectious and spread.

Can you see the foreshadowing of the work of the Messiah in the above Scriptures? Do you recognize Him in the midst of those thorns? Words fail to express how grateful I am for the Lord taking those ugly, sin-twisted thorns upon His brow for us. Have you ever stopped to imagine how painful this was for the Messiah?

If you have ever seen a thorn bush, you can picture how these very long needle-like objects pierced His head and caused blood to flow. I imagine the area was like my arm, only intensified one hundred fold, all red, hot and swollen. Inflammation was over His weary eyes. And this would only be the beginning of the pain He would endure as He took one consequence after another for our sins.

Are you in a place where it seems you are surrounded by thorns? You are laboring in the field of souls, but it seems the lilies fail to spring up, and all you see are the thorns and thistles. Take heart, my dear one. The Lord has already taken the scourge of the thorns upon Himself. He took all the payment for our sin. Eventually, as you continue to work toward the harvest, beautiful souls will blossom there. Every place your feet shall tread shall be blessed for His sake.

Further Along the Way

Looking through the above Scriptures in Genesis, can you see clearly that thorns were a consequence for Adam and Eve's sin? Have you ever struggled with thinking it unfair that all creation suffered for the sin of original man?

In my story, I told of a time I was hurt by thorns. I correlated that with brushing up against sin and only seeing and feeling the pain later on. We have all sinned, even as believers. Think of your own life. Recount the times when you sinned and it seemed harmless at first, but then the pain occurred. How may you prevent this horrible cycle?

My hope is that you have a deeper understanding of the sacrifice of Jesus. Spend some time giving Him thanks for the thorns He willingly took for your sake.

Are there areas in your life where you see thorns instead of lilies? List people you have prayed for. Now give praise to the Lord, in faith, for His raising up those souls to Himself.

Father help us to see that we do not need to fear the consequences of sin. Thank You for sending Your Son to pay that debt. Help us to serve You in gratitude for this great gift of salvation. May we keep pressing forward, never losing hope for lilies in exchange for thorns.

Remember Me

"And he was saying, 'Jesus, remember me when You come in Your kingdom!' And He said to him, 'Truly I say to you, today you shall be with Me in Paradise.'" Luke 23:42,43

When I was living in South Africa, we had Bible study with some precious elder ladies in town. They would pray for Nancy Hudson, a missionary friend, and myself often. They would ask about our families as well. When I would prepare to visit home, the ladies would say, "Remember me to your parents." To the American English speaker, this might seem a strange thing to say. But after living with a people group for a while, you begin to understand their way of thinking. "Remember me to your parents" was their way of saying, "Mention me to your parents, and let them know I am mindful of them."

Remember me—we all desire to be remembered, and we hope we are remembered in a good light. Most want to change for the better. That's why there are so many New Year's resolutions. Can I speak a truth to you which may radically change your way of living? Our new beginning, our better plan, our new strength, our light breaking forth from darkness, begins at the cross. The Scripture above is a reminder of this. There were two thieves on crosses next to Jesus. The crowd was hurling all kinds of insults at the Lord as He hung there torn from head to toe. The darkness of all the ages was descending on His body as He took all sin to Himself that day. And out of that dark place of jeering from the crowds, a voice called out to Him for mercy.

The voice no doubt was faint, yet desperate. The thief was hanging there looking and listening. He saw the Prince of Peace for His soul. He saw his only salvation, while others were missing it. And what words does he utter with his last dying breath? "Jesus, remember me when You come in Your Kingdom!"

Be assured this morning as you meet the year ahead just as the thief was assured that dark day in history. The Light of Christ was with Him, and He is with us as well. Jesus forgave that thief that day and promised him salvation. He promises the same to you and me. For the thief, he received a brand new life. We, too, are living in the power of eternity. As the thief looked to the Messiah on the cross for his salvation, let's also remember the cross today. This will be our new beginning. This is our new life. The power of the cross broke through that day. The ground shook. The dead were raised. The veil was torn.

Wherever you are in this day, Jesus says, "Remember me, I am here for you. I will shake the ground on your behalf. I will remove the veil of doubt from your eyes and give you new vision. I will raise your mortal bodies to health!"

Further Along the Way

All over the globe people want to be remembered in a good light. That's why headstones are so fancy. When this life is over, what would you desire people to remember about you most? What would you write on your own headstone?

Our new beginning, our better plan, our new strength, our breaking forth from darkness begins at the cross." What does this mean? How can you begin to apply this truth to your own life?

Whatever you desire to be remembered for has deep meaning. Could it perhaps say much about your relationship with Christ? With other people?

The thief on the cross had one plea—remember me when you get into your kingdom. Do you think this sinner had a deeper desire? What was he really crying out for?

Has Jesus' response caused you to realize how greatly loved you are? In His greatest sorrow when He was taking His last breath, He ministered to a common sinner like us. If you are grateful for this love, make a list of five other common sinners you can share this story of the thief on the cross with.

Father, help us to cry out to You like the thief on the cross did when our world is the darkest. Let us strive to be remembered as ones who have loved You and have pointed others to You.

I Hope You Dance

"With a leap he stood upright and began to walk; and he entered the temple with them, walking and leaping and praising God." Acts 3:8

There probably isn't anything more heartbreaking than to hear the cries of a child who is in excruciating pain, but that was my sister, Annmarie, and her husband, Rob's experience for weeks at Boston Children's Hospital. My baby niece, Ella Rose, as mentioned earlier, had undergone a bone marrow transplant, and her immunities were so low that a virus attacked her liver. She was horribly bloated, as her body gained ten pounds of water weight. She was in intensive care and cried day and night, calling for her Mommy. But her mother could not hold her because she was in too much pain for touch. My sister was usually pretty hopeful, but the voice over the phone was depleted of any emotions. Her emotions and her body were drained. "We're believing the Lord for a miracle, Ann" was all I could say, as my own voice was cracking from exhaustion. We'd cried our hearts out for this baby to be healed for months now, and every time she took a few steps forward, there was a set-back.

Weeks passed and finally there was a breakthrough. Her liver was picking up momentum, and she was out of danger. She had far to go, however. She was still pretty weak. My sister and I spoke again, and she gave me a breakdown of the details of her liver function. I was hopeful and said, "Ann, I'm praying Ella dances."

That following morning after the phone conversation with my sister, I got up early to pray as usual. I began to pray and remind the Lord of His promise to bring this baby through. I said, "Lord, I pray she dances." It was a tall order I know, but to me her dancing meant she was well. The Lord dropped this into my spirit, *then dance for Ella.*

My heart was pumping now. I knew I had to dance for Ella in faith believing that she would soon dance. I picked up an 8x10 picture I had of her. I held that baby's picture to my chest, and I began to dance. I twirled around and sang as loud as I could, praising the Lord for what He was about to do. I felt the anointing reach down into my living room. I knew Ella would dance.

Each day I'd ask, "Is she dancing yet?" My sister would reply, "No, not yet." One morning my sister said, "I put her princess dress on her, but she would have no part of dancing." Days can seem eternal when you are waiting for a healing. But finally the baby got up one day. She had her Elmo tape on and she began to dance! I knew then the Lord had done a mighty work, and she would be well because she finally danced.

In the above Scripture, a man who was lame from birth was healed. Instantly, he got up, began to walk, leap and praise God. This to me is a wonderful example of a complete healing. He didn't just get up and begin to stumble and walk. He was leaping and praising. Sounds like a dance to me. He was rejoicing so deeply that he couldn't contain himself. The word *rejoice* actually means to spin around wildly and lose control. You can sense his excitement and his joy. But it wasn't always this way for that man at the gate. He was begging daily, and it had become routine for him. He saw the apostles coming toward him, and he began asking for alms (money). He never dreamed to ask to walk. Peter and John were not satisfied to leave him in this state. This was going to be a new day for this man. They commanded him saying, "Look at us!" They then told him that they had no money but had something much more valuable and necessary. They proclaimed Jesus to the man and told him to walk in the name of Jesus Christ, the Nazarene. He did. He walked, he leapt, and he praised God.

Just as the apostles were not satisfied to leave the man motionless, I was not satisfied to see my niece, Ella, lying there alive but motionless in that hospital bed. I wanted to see her dance. Dancing to me says *it is well*.

I believe we all need to ask for more than survival. We need to put feet to our prayers and walk them through literally. Just as I picked up that baby's picture and danced with her as though she were with me, we all need to believe God for great things. He is waiting for us to test Him, to remind Him of His promises for us.

I hope you dance. I pray you dance. I believe you can dance. Yes, dance like no one is watching, but be blessed knowing that the God of the universe actually sees your every move. And as you dance, believe Him for mighty works.

Further Along the Way

Has there been times in your life when you were just hanging on? Were you satisfied to ask the Lord to help you survive, not considering asking for more? Thinking back on those times, what more could you have asked for? Make a list of several such circumstances and then also list what more you desired the Lord to do but were afraid to ask.

In addition to the Scripture above, look up Psalm 63:5. It clearly states that when we praise the Lord a transformation happens in our countenance. Praise brings great joy. Can you see a correlation here when I danced for Ella and her body and spirit were both lifted?

Can you think of a time when you praised the Lord in a trial and others were touched because of your praise? Consider situations you are going through now. List them. Ask the Lord to move abundantly in those areas of need. Is there someone who needs salvation? Start singing in faith, believing they will one day sing praises themselves. Is it finances? Believe the Lord to direct you to financial freedom as well as abundance so that you can bless others. Is it healing? Get your dancing shoes on and dance in faith believing your loved one will dance both in body and spirit.

Lastly, look again to the Scripture in Acts 3. The man was so excited he couldn't contain himself. Do you believe sometimes we do not remain well because we easily forget what the Lord has done? Do you think praise has the power to keep us well in body and spirit?

Father, You alone are able to set us free. Lord, make us dance.

He Calls You Lily

"I am the rose of Sharon, the lily of the valley. Like a lily among the thorns, so is my darling among the maidens." Song of Solomon 2:1-2

As I walk into her father's church, I see her dancing and twirling about. She is three and has no reservations as she bounces with glee. She is as cute as a button, my little Lily Pad—that is my nickname for her, although her parents call her Lily. She is always a welcomed sight, and I am sure many agree she warms the soul as they walk into the Lord's presence, for she is a Lily amongst thorns.

Any given Sunday morning you can enter many churches and see lilies as they reflect the freedom of Jesus. They are the ones who are liberated in His love. They dance with gusto. Even though they are surrounded by thorns, they pay no mind.

Lilies speak of purity and beauty. They are the ones who carry Christ's love and water the rest of the body of believers with that love. When the Scripture above speaks of the lily, it is speaking of those who have been liberated by the love of Christ. It states, "Like a lily among thorns, so is my darling among the maidens." Here Solomon is speaking about the love of his life. Interestingly enough, just before these words, He describes himself in the same way. He is the lily of the valley. Those who study the Word know that Solomon here represents Christ. He is drawing His Bride. He is telling her that she is beautiful, and He sees a reflection of Himself when He looks at her. Compared to the other plants of the meadow, she is as a rose or lily among thorns—those diseased ones that are all snarled, twisted and ugly. They are prickly, abrasive and can do much harm.

The Messiah was the ultimate rose or lily among thorns. Think of Him throughout His life battling with the religious leaders of His time. They were abrasive, hard-hearted and when He got close to them, they desired to pierce Him through. These thorns were intent on killing not only Him but the spirit of freedom He demonstrated. They went as far as conspiring to the very piercing of His hands, feet and side.

Jesus hung on the cross right in the middle of two thorns. They were common criminals. It was for the thorns He came into the world. As the Rose of Sharon breathed His last, one thorn swayed toward Him. The sacrificial love of the Messiah was drawing Him and as he asked the Lord to remember him, his thorny heart was changed. How could this common thief ever imagine that in mere moments he would become like the one he was looking on. As the petals of the Rose of Sharon, Yeshua, were crushed that day, the love of the Father splashed all over that sinner. That thorn became a lily.

Perhaps you enter a house of worship and see lilies. They are dancing freely, but it somehow offends you. Yet, at the same time, you wish you could be freer. Could it be there are thorns in your life? Are you somehow like the religious leaders, and your heart has become hardened? Attending a place of worship has become tradition for you. You judge any movement of freedom as flesh, and you determine not to enter in.

There is freedom for all of us. Those thorns do not have to pain you any longer. Come to the crushed rose, the Messiah. Allow His sweet fragrance to heal you today. Embrace the lilies He has sent you and learn from them.

Further Along the Way

How does the text give you a clearer picture of Jesus being the Lily of the valley? Name some times when there were thorns in your life, those times when life seemed to prick and pierce right through you. Do you remember how you came out of those situations? Do you see Jesus as the Lily splashing His love all over you?

Do you have Lilies in your church? As they freely worship in dance, how does this make you feel? If it makes you uncomfortable, could it be you are lacking freedom? Close your eyes and try to imagine Jesus dancing as He did. Now ask Him to fill you with the freedom He longs to give you.

Father, You sent Your Son to be crushed under the weight of our sins. Help us to receive what He has done. May we become Your lilies, reflecting the love of the Messiah.

Window Shopping

"My beloved is like a gazelle or a young stag. Behold, he is standing behind our wall, He is looking through the windows, He is peering through the lattice." Song of Solomon 2:9

I remember my young days as a believer. I was so in love. I wanted everything the Lord Jesus had for me. One day, I was praying and feeling very bold. I remember pleading, "Lord, show me your glory." My hands were raised high. But almost instantly a holy fear came upon me. I fell to my knees. My plea turned to, "No Lord, I'm not ready!" I don't know what I thought I would see, but whatever His glory looked like scared me that day. I imagined if the Lord showed me a hint of His glory, I would come totally undone, much like the prophet Isaiah.

Now that I am a more seasoned believer, I realize I have seen His glory. In the above Scripture, the writer is referring to her lover. Yet, it is well known that lover is pointing to Jesus. The Scripture states, "Behold, He is standing behind our wall, He is looking through the windows." Believe it or not, I have seen Him peering at me through the windows in a literal way.

I have shared about my niece, Ella Rose, having a bone marrow transplant. She was in isolation for a year following three blows with death. Our family couldn't go near her or touch her for several months following her return home. It was winter time and we had to stand outside her window, and she would peer out at us. To her, it was a little game; she was receiving visitors. I would stand there freezing cold and jump up and down just to see her smile. I didn't mind the cold toes. I wanted to be there so she knew I cared. I wanted just a glimpse of this child.

Although I was in her presence, the window was a barrier. It protected her from my germs. It would have been dangerous for me to come any closer to her. I could see with my eyes all the Lord had done. His glory was shining through that window. And that had to be enough until His work of healing in Ella Rose was complete.

Experiencing the glory of the Lord is like this. We get little glimpses. We may get goose bumps, but we can only come so close. The Scripture tells us that we see through a glass dimly. Just as the window and the screen blocked my vision of my niece a little, we see Jesus for the time being through filters. We don't see Him in His full glory. We see enough of the glory to get us through our current experience, but as time goes by and we spend more time with Him, we become more and more able to stand and experience a keener vision of Him.

Although we can only see Him dimly, the above Scripture goes on to say, "He is looking through the windows, He is peering through the lattice." I love that. The lattice is made of a heavy material with little spaces. Can you imagine the Messiah looking through? He's watching out for us.

We all go through experiences where we need to see the glory of the Lord. Be encouraged. He is moving on our behalf. There are barriers in our hearts, but He is breaking down walls and causing spaces where His love and glory can shine through.

Further Along the Way

Do you remember when you first came to Christ? Were you like me in the story, anxious to see His glory? Do you think it is wise to be a little fearful of seeing that glory?

What did maturity cause me to realize later on? The above Scripture states that He is looking through the window. How does this apply to our lives? I shared about Ella Rose and how I now know the Lord was showing His glory as I got a glimpse of her in the window. Can you recount at least three experiences where you have known the Lord was manifesting His glory to you in a real way?

I mention filters or barriers to our hearts which block us seeing His glory fully. Do you see such barriers in your own heart? All who love Jesus desire to see His glory; however, we are only given a little vision at a time. Could it be possible this is for our own protection? What could he be protecting us from?

Does the fact that we see enough glory to get us through bring you comfort? Consider how you can comfort others with this.

Father, sometimes we run all over looking for Your glory to appear. Give us the faith to see Your glory already manifested in our lives.

A Compassionate Father

"Just as a father has compassion on his children, so the Lord has compassion on those who fear Him. He Himself knows our frame; He is mindful that we are but dust." Psalm 103:13-14

Have you ever watched a parent have patience with their toddler or a parent disciplining a young child or teenager? Sometimes parent/child relationships amaze me. Some cause me to praise the Lord and some, well to be honest, cause me to cringe. In my line of work, I see and hear both kinds of interactions.

I have no biological children, of course, so that makes me the *best* parent (I'm snickering). Even though I have none of my own, I have had many experiences with children. Here is a truth I have found—good parenting takes much patience. It also takes huge amounts of maturity and wisdom. A parent who demonstrates healthy discipline is aware of a child's development and gages their behavior with that knowledge. On the flip side of the coin, unhealthy discipline comes when the parent expects the child to be an adult. They fail to remember what makes a toddler a toddler, a young child a young child, and a teenager a teenager. In healthy parenting, no one realizes what their child is made up of more than the parent. All the expectations of behavior come from that knowledge.

In the Scripture above, the Lord Himself knows our frame. Why is this so important to understand? He is our perfect Parent. He alone knows all we are made of. When we feel down or feel like we have failed miserably, we as believers sometimes want to pull away from the Father's love in fear or shame. However, the Father remembers our frame. He remembers that you and I are only dust. Because of this, He deals with us accordingly. Do you realize you are often more harsh on yourself than He is?

The Scripture above says, "Just as a father has compassion on his children, so the Lord has compassion on those who fear Him." When you and I mess up and really feel as though we have failed, He looks at us and remembers, "I have made them from the dust of the earth." We will remain in this condition until we see Jesus face to face. Then we will be complete in the Spirit and in His likeness.

Until then, come before the Father in boldness, realizing that His compassion for you is enough to get you to where He desires you to be. His compassion sent Him to the cross; your sin has already been paid for. His Word says He has compassion on those who fear Him. Those who reverence Him, who know who He is, have a healthy fear, not a cowering fear.

Further Along the Way

Look back at your life. Can you count at least five times you failed the Lord miserably? Now try to recall how you behaved after failing Him. Did you pull away each time?

How can the above Scripture, which states He is a compassionate Father, help you deal with failure in the future?

Our Father is compassionate, merciful, and perfect in His dealings with us. Meditate on His character this week.

Lord, I often feel I have failed in this life. I know some of my sisters and brothers feel the same at times. You are perfect in Your dealings with Your children. I thank You that You remember we are only made of dust. Help us to see ourselves as redeemed and to forgive others and remember what they are made of as we deal with them.

Be on Watch

"And He said to them, 'My soul is deeply grieved to the point of death; remain here and keep watch. And He came and found them sleeping, and said to Peter, 'Simon, are you asleep? Could you not keep watch for one hour?'" Mark 14:34, 37

I read much of what my friends write on face book, but I rarely respond. I am usually pretty careful if I do respond because if I went with impulse, I might offend a few. This morning as I was reading, I saw that a friend had written how someone said something flippant, and it obviously caused pain. This person is going through a very painful and trying time as she watches her dad go through cancer treatment.

Watch. Jesus in the above Scriptures tells His disciples that His soul is deeply grieved to the point of death. He asks His disciples to watch and pray and when He returns, He finds them sleeping within an hour.

Friends, let me share this. When someone is grieving to the point of death, we who love that person need to *watch*. Watch what we say and how we say it. Watch means to be guarded. The disciples were told to watch because there was danger ahead for Jesus. We, as believers, are also called to watch out for our friends when they are in sorrow. There is a real danger that offenses could lead to stumbling in someone's walk.

When my niece was seemingly close to death during a bone marrow transplant, people were on the watch for her and our family. They prayed for her until the Lord moved on her behalf. Most watched and prayed and said only positive and encouraging words, but one person said something very negative and even alarming. People can be very insensitive. That person's words could have caused me to stumble. However, for that one person's negative words, there were hundreds "watching and praying" that were only positive and healing.

As you go along today my friends, be on the *watch* and be on guard for your brothers and sisters in the faith. Let nothing careless or hurtful fall from your lips. Use your words to heal and not bring down. Let's stay vigilant and alert on our posts for the sake of those who are in sorrow and need of prayer.

Further Along the Way

We all speak too quickly at times. Can you think of just one time this week when you could have been more sensitive to another person? Perhaps you might think it necessary to ask their forgiveness.

I mentioned our experience while praying my niece through a transplant. Someone spoke a negative and insensitive remark. In what way could this have hurt my family? Do you believe someone else's negative or insensitive attitude can influence the way other's pray? Do others effect how we approach God in prayer?

What do you believe is the biggest danger in us not keeping watch for one another?

Take some time and seek the Lord in prayer as to how you can be more alert while watching. List some of the ways He makes clear to you. Share those with a prayer partner.

Father forgive us for being lax at times. We fail to see the dangers of sleeping when we should be vigilant. Give us a heart focused on You. Prick our spirits to be on alert for one another.

Jesus Lights Our Way

"I have come as Light into the world, so that everyone who believes in Me will not remain in darkness." John 12:46

Are you at a loss as to what to do in a situation? Do you pray asking the Lord to remove the situation or to move in a certain circumstance you are facing? You pray and pray and nothing seems to be changing. Perhaps you are praying amiss. Perhaps the problem is you need to ask the Lord what *you* need to do in a situation. "Lord, what is *my* part? What would You have *me* to do?"

The Scripture above states Jesus is the Light of the world. He came as Light so those of us who follow Him would not stumble, trip, and walk aimlessly through life's troubles. He brings perfect direction. In my mind's eye, I see Jesus walking ahead of someone. He is brilliant Light. As the person walks closer and closer, His Light shines brightly and casts its light on them. They cannot remain in the dark because His Light has come into their path, and they are surrounded by brightness. The way has been made clear.

Are you in the dark about a seemingly impossible situation? Follow closely. Ask the Lord to show you what you must do. Walking closely with the Lord Jesus is truly the only way to make your path clear. Counsel from other areas pale significantly to His brilliance. The Bible says, "His Word is a lamp unto my feet and a light unto my path."

I recently had a situation that was hurtful. I truly was at a loss of how to handle it. I had to ask the Lord, "What is my part in this? What must I do to bring reconciliation?" He showed me I had to ask forgiveness for my part and also offer forgiveness. The outcome I hoped for did not happen; however, I feel free now to brush off the dust, the heaviness of this burden. I am also free to continue to pray for the other person's heart to be healed.

The Lord offers us all freedom to walk as He desires us to—in His Light. As we do, the darkness of this world will have no power to defeat us. Rather, we will become that beacon of light others so desperately need on their path, and we will lead them to Christ.

Further Along the way

Do you think sometimes we pray missing the mark? Why do you think the Lord might prefer us to ask what our part is when He has the power to change everything?

Why do you feel the Lord refers to Himself as the Light of the world?

Sometimes we really are at a loss as to what to do to be fair and just in a situation. Do you think these times are some of what the Scripture refers to as darkness?

God's Word is a lamp unto our feet the psalmist states in Psalm 119. What could this possibly mean?

Why do you think the Lord freed me to "brush the dust off"? Do you think we sometimes stumble because we are weighed down from carrying the heaviness on our own?

What is an added benefit to walking in the light as stated in the text?

Father, help us to remember not to walk aimlessly but to ask for wisdom so we are no longer in darkness.

I Hold You?

"Draw me after you and let us run together! The King has brought me into his chambers. We will rejoice in you and be glad; we will extol your love more than wine. Rightly do they love you." Song of Solomon 1:4

When my niece, Ella Rose, was a toddler, we used to go on wonderful walks together. Ella Rose had just come through a life threatening illness, and her immunities were low. She was in isolation for close to a year, and now she was free to see the outside. Oh, the joy on this child's face was contagious. I loved her excitement at everything in her path.

Ella would shout to me, "Come, Aunt Wauie. I chase you!" And then she would run away from me because she really meant for me to be chasing her. I would just giggle and play along with her. After all the hurt this child had gone through, I would do anything to see her full of joy.

One time I was chasing her and true to her age, she stumbled over her own feet and fell. Her laughter and glee turned quickly to tears. I ran over and picked her up for a second, dusted her off, and we began to walk again. I had just had cancer surgery myself and wasn't supposed to lift her. She was 34 lbs. by then. In less than a few moments later, Ella hugged my legs and looked up at me. Her big brown eyes were full of tears. "Aunt Wauie, I hold you?" I knew what she meant. She needed comfort. She was hurting and wanted her stronger, loving Aunt Wauie to hold her. My heart melted as she searched my face for an answer. Of course, I picked her up and held her tight. She snuggled her little face in my neck and that's how we walked home. I love this child so much, I could never deny her. She could have asked me for the moon that day, and I would have tried my best to get it for her.

Since Adam and Eve sinned in the garden, there has been a separation between man and his Creator. Even if we are not aware of it, our heart's cry is, "Draw me." Just as my niece was hurting and wanted someone stronger than herself to hold her close, we too desire the same.

The above Scripture states, "Draw me after you and let us run together!" If you have ever been in love you realize that there is a chasing that goes on. You chase after the object of your affection. You want to hold that person and demonstrate how deeply you love them. You also desire that person to want to hold you.

The Scripture above goes on to say, "The King has brought me into His inner chamber." The inner chamber here represents a private dwelling place or secret place. According to Psalm 91, He who dwells in the secret place of the Most High shall abide in the shadow of the Almighty. What comforting words these are.

A true test of a love relationship is the amount of effort you are willing to put into it. If we are in relationships where only one person is doing the chasing, then it's unhealthy. This is true in our relationship to Jesus as well. Jesus has already called us to Himself. He has demonstrated His love for us in the most severe manner. He paid the bride's price by actually dying for us, therefore, proving He loved us more than He loved His own life. Try to get that into your spirit. Let it register deep in your being. This truth will cancel any fear of being worthless. You are valuable. He paid the greatest price possible for you.

Furthermore, in healthy relationships, we can do nothing to make a person love us more. Their love is unconditional. The same is true of Jesus. He moved wind and wave to prove His love for us. However, how we react to His love, has no bearing on how much He loves us. He loves those who reject Him just as much as He loves those who receive Him. How are we sure? The Scriptures tell us so—"While we were yet sinners He loved us" and "God so loved the world that he gave His only begotten Son." As you know, the whole world doesn't receive His love and yet He died for them, as well.

Ask yourself today, are you deeply in love with Jesus? Are you chasing after Him? Are you longing for Him to hold you? Is this relationship exclusive? We all have other relationships in life. That is how we are wired. However, this relationship between you and Christ has to be set apart. It's holy. It's unique. It has to be above all others. I love my Peanut, Ella Rose, to the moon and back. I might even be willing to lay down my life for her if necessary. However, even my love for her pales in comparison to my love for Christ. He completes me. He is who I run to when I need comfort.

The wonder of it all is Jesus will continue to love us no matter how we return that love. Yet, if we are not pursuing Him as a lover, we will always have a holy longing that will go unsatisfied.

Join me today. Look into the face of Christ and ask, "I hold you?" I know He will hold you close and walk with you.

Further Along the Way

We all have people we love deeply. Sometimes we are like my little niece, Ella Rose. We desire the other person to chase us. We often test that love. The acid test of love is always behavior. How did Jesus pass this test? What behavior proved beyond doubt His great love for us?

Scripture states love casts out fear. What fears do you think you hold on to which His love proves unnecessary? If you are like me, I often struggle with the fear of being worthless and rejected. Try to focus on the great price the Lord paid for you. Do you now see that you are valuable?

The above Scripture says, "Draw me after you and let us run together." Is this your heart's cry? Ask the Lord to draw you. Ask Him to show you anything which is coming between you and Him.

Father, help us all to draw closer to the Lover of our souls. Your love is amazing. Thank You

A Tale of Two Sisters

"Now the Angel of the Lord found her by a spring of water in the wilderness, by the spring on the way to Shur." Genesis 16:7

Nazeem came to my office in tears most days. Such a beautiful young lady with almond eyes, dark hair and olive skin. Tears somehow seemed out of place; she was young, intelligent and about to be married. So what was her great concern? Why all the tears you might wonder.

Unlike most brides, she was about to marry a man she didn't love. She was of Egyptian descent and living in a foreign land. Because her parents were poor and desperate, they accepted a generous bride's price for their daughter. Nazeem's heart was breaking. It wasn't so much that she found the man unattractive or even that he wasn't very nice. There was something much deeper concerning her. Romance had little to do with it. Her family ties were stronger than girlish romance. In her culture, family loyalty was everything. You see, it was the still, small voice that concerned her most. Unlike Nazeem's peers, she had given her life to Jesus recently, and this man she was offered to was not only a non-believer, He was of a faith which had persecuted many she knew. How could she become one with a man who denied all she lived for?

In our culture today, it's difficult for us to fully understand Nazeem's dilemma. However, in some cultures, to disobey your parents is considered a great and even grave offence. She'd bring shame to her whole family, and therefore, she would be alienated. Nazeem's parents had already accepted the bride's price, It was their ticket out of poverty. *Sold* was written all over Nazeem. So what was she to do?

Because we were in a dangerous region, I was forbidden to offer counsel, which might influence Nazeem to go against her parent's decision. So each day we were together, we would pray. One day she was crying so hard, I felt my own heart breaking. I was also desperate for an answer. As we were praying, I felt I should ask, "Nazeem, what does the Scripture tell you?" Her reply, "I should not be unevenly yoked, for what fellowship does light have with darkness?" We looked at each other and knew she had her answer. I encouraged her to press on.

As our ministry prepared to leave, my parting words to her were, "Nazeem, Jesus is faithful. He has promised to provide for all your needs, and He will never leave you." I knew trust was of the essence for Nazeem. Although everything looked impossible, I continued to pray for her.

Upon my return to America, I found a letter from Nazeem. I anxiously opened it. The letter read: "I have put my trust totally in our Savior Jesus Christ. I took a stand and refused to marry that man. Jesus made a way. I am working a good job now and helping support my parents. I am paying the bride's price back. Now I attend a big church, and the people love me and support me. Jesus is faithful, and I love Him too much!"—Nazeem.

Nazeem's journey reminds me of another Egyptian woman—Hagar. She was sold to a family and living in a foreign land. Her mistress abused her. Hagar was desperate for an answer. Alone and running in the wilderness, she quieted herself long enough to hear a still, small voice. It was the Angel of the Lord saying, "You will have a son, and his name will be Ishmael."

Ishmael means, "God Hears." The message to Hagar was the Lord has heard of your misery. The Lord promised Hagar her descendants would be more than could be counted. What a promise to a woman who must have felt so alone. The Lord knew that even in her descendants, the Arab peoples, He would have a remnant.

As with Hagar and Nazeem, He promises us, "I will never leave you nor forsake you. I am the God of the impossible." The Lord would have you remember He is the Lord your God, merciful, gracious, longsuffering and abounding in goodness. There is nothing too difficult for Him.

Further Along the Way

What is your impossible situation? Are you in a place you never imagined you would be? Like both Nazeem and Hagar, does it seem you are alone in this struggle?

In my story, Nazeem was in a seemingly impossible circumstance and yet the Lord rescued her. Do you honestly believe He can do the same in your situation?

What were Nazeem's biggest concerns? Do you see a major difference in our culture compared with hers? How do you see that her concerns are actually Biblically sound?

Look back in the text. How did the Lord answer her heart's cry for help?

After reading this account of a missionary's dilemma, do you have a greater understanding of what missionaries might be up against as they share Christ in foreign culture? As a believer, how might you be a help to your church's missionaries?

Father, You alone know all the times we feel so abandoned by others. You see all those seemingly impossible situations. Help us to remember You see, hear and answer according to Your great purposes. You do the impossible.

Running Wild

"Are not five sparrows sold for two cents? Yet not one of them is forgotten before God. Indeed, the very hairs of your head are all numbered. Do not fear; you are more valuable than many sparrows." Luke 12: 6-7

Yesterday, just before our program began, one of the little girls fell and got hurt. She was running full speed in the school hall and fell hard on her knee. The nurse cared for her and after icing her knee, she was a little shaken but fine.

During group time, I went over to her as she was nursing her knee with it still propped up. I asked her how she felt and if her knee still hurt. It was better; in fact, she wanted to begin running again. This is something we have spoken about many times, as we meet in the cafeteria and the floors are hard. They are not to run all over. I reminded her of this. "This is why Ms. Laurie asks you not to run in school. I don't want you to get hurt." She became weepy and said, "Ms. Laurie, I was running because I thought if you didn't see me you would leave me." I assured her that would never happen. If she were not with the group, I would come looking for her.

Some of us have the same thoughts as this seven year old at times. We think we have to run all over and get the Lord's attention or the attention of others. We fear we will be forgotten somehow. Haven't you ever felt this way? Or haven't you seen someone else light up with joy and surprise when you noticed them missing from some function?

So many people struggle with fears of abandonment. Unfortunately, because we are surrounded by other humans, there will always be uncertainties in relationships. We will be rejected by others at times. And let's be honest. We sometimes reject others in need. It's the human condition.

But we will *never* be abandoned by the Lord Jesus. He has promised to never leave us nor forsake us. He is the Good Shepherd. When one of His sheep is missing from the fold, He looks for them. Actually, He knows their every move, and He pulls them back in with His love.

Just as my seven year old student had to learn not to run in fear of being left, we have to learn not to run all over and trust He will be waiting for us. He's looking out for us.

Fellow pilgrim, be encouraged. A sparrow doesn't fall without His knowing, and you are worth much more than a thousand sparrows. He paid the greatest price for you.

Further Along the Way

Abandonment is such a prevalent issue today. Globally, a great number of people do not even know their fathers. Why do you think this is?

Can you reflect to your own childhood and remember times you felt abandoned, perhaps even by your own parents?

Our earthly fathers are to be examples of Father God's love. Can you see a correlation between fatherless homes and people not trusting God as a loving father? Do you believe abandonment has a direct effect on society?

The Scripture states when your father and mother forsake you, the Lord never does. Why should this bring much comfort?

The above Scripture states we are more valuable than many sparrows. How did the Lord Jesus prove this statement to be true? What great price did He pay for you?

Now consider those in your inner circle of family and friends. Do you sense they are struggling with issues of rejection or fears of being abandoned? Look back at the text and Scripture. How could you assure them? List ways to assure them they are not alone.

Father, You take such good care of us. We are never out of Your sight or care. Help us to trust You, running less and resting more.

Feeling Stuck

"My eyes are continually toward the Lord, for He will pluck my feet out of the net. Turn to me and be gracious to me, for I am lonely and afflicted." Psalm 25: 15-16

Do you sometimes feel "stuck" or "trapped"? The psalmist, David, knew these feelings all too well. It seems he was always on the run from his enemies. He says his "eyes are continually towards the Lord." He believes His God will eventually rescue him. He asks the Lord to be gracious to him. He is alone and afflicted.

Be gracious the psalmist says. What could this mean? Is it not enough for the Lord to come and rescue? Here David is asking, "Please Lord, whatever it takes to set me free. I trust you. Be gracious. Do not let your servant be put to shame."

"For I am lonely and afflicted"—isn't this how we feel at times in our struggles? We may not even be alone. We have family and friends who love us. We are on prayer lists, but we *feel* alone and afflicted. I believe there are times in life when certain struggles cause a person to truly feel alone in their battle. They trust Jesus. They appreciate their family and friends, but this season in their journey is lonely. Let's face it. Some trials in life have similarities; that's why support groups are so wonderful. But no deep trial is exactly alike because God has an individual plan for each person. Not only is the struggle unique, but the heart fashioned for this struggle is also unique. Our struggles and hearts are custom fit for the plan of the Master.

In the end, all who continually look to the Lord, as the David did, will become the Lord's Masterpiece. We are God's masterpieces in the making. He is the Master-builder, and He is building us all up for His pleasure. Just think on this. The Creator of the universe is taking pleasure in *you*—His masterpiece.

Further Along the Way

Do you feel stuck or trapped at times? What is your first response when feeling these emotions? Now look at the verses above. How did the psalmist respond?

David was often running from enemies. He was a powerful warrior, yet even he felt trapped or stuck. He had so many who praised him, and still he felt alone in his affliction. Do you sometimes feel as David? Your family and friends are surrounding you; however, feeling alone plagues you. Look to the text. Why do you think this is happening?

Is it safe to say those who love the Lord sometimes feel alone? They have great faith, yet their feelings of loneliness are valid. Do you agree with my observation that some trials are specifically picked by the Master for His Master plan in our lives?

Can you recall others in Scripture who went through trials, looked to the Lord, and were not put to shame? I will give you one—the woman caught in adultery. The men desired to bring her much shame and even death. However, Jesus extended love and grace. How does this encourage you?

Ask the Lord to show you three people you can be in prayer for who are going through trials and feel alone.

Father, as I write these words I am reminded of ordinary people in Scripture who felt alone and afflicted. You touched their lives, and You did not shame them while doing so. Thank You for being gracious to those who call on You. I'm also mindful of those who face seemingly impossible trials. They feel stuck or trapped. Even though they are surrounded by others, they feel alone in their affliction. Lord, wrap Yourself around them now. Give them just a glimpse of the masterpiece You are working in them—enough to keep them going, Lord. Stir us all to pray for our brothers and sisters in their time of great trial. Give us a heart like Yours. In Jesus' Name, amen.

Fashioned Hearts

"From His dwelling place He looks out on all the inhabitants of the earth, He who fashions the hearts of them all, He understands all their works." Psalm 33:15

We have all been misjudged by someone and have also misjudged others. The Scripture tells us to judge not lest we be judged; however, it also says to judge the fruit of others—"You will know them by their fruit." So, is the Scripture contradicting itself? *Never, ever* does Scripture contradict itself. How can truth lie?

If we look at the above verse, we may get some answers. The Lord of all creation looks out from His dwelling place and sees all the inhabitants of the earth. Let's try to get a handle on just this for a moment. You and I experience world affairs through the media, which is mostly tainted at best. Few of us have traveled and perhaps experienced other lands and other people and their situations. Yet, the Lord Almighty has the ability to see *all* at all times. He sees everywhere each and every person has walked. He sees every expression, whether that of pain or joy. He has heard every thought made deep in the heart of *all* man before it is even spoken out loud. He hears every cry of a child who is left abandoned or abused. He sees the consequences of that abuse as it unfolds in that young life.

Get this reality in your spirit. He who made the heavens and the earth and way beyond fashioned each and every heart of all mankind. To fashion means there was a plan. He took amazing care. He had a future planned out for every heart.

My heart was not fashioned like yours and nor yours like mine. Therefore, my steps are ordained to take a very different path than yours. All our steps are prepared before us by a loving purposeful God, and yet, life happens. Relationships happen. Wrong teachings are received. Life experiences take that fashioned heart and damage it at times. Each heartache is unique to the way a person has been fashioned. That's why one person reacts to abuse or neglect in a totally different way than another person experiencing something very similar. We see this in siblings. They grow up with the same parents and experiences, but later on their lifestyles can be remarkably different.

What am I getting at? We can judge a person's fruit, meaning their behaviors, to be righteous or sinful. Sin is sin. If you know right from wrong, you can rightfully judge what is sinful in a person's life, while being aware of the sin in your own life. However, and please hear this, you and I cannot judge the heart of man. We did not fashion his heart, and we lack understanding of its workings. Only God Who put that heart together and molded it, fashioned it, and wired the person's personality to fit that exact heart and purpose can rightfully judge it. He is judge.

I get this question all the time. Was so and so saved? Let me say this. I may look at so and so's life and see bad behavior and think they do not know the Lord. However, only the Lord knows if that person is coming to Him and repenting and seeking strength to get out of their sin. Jesus is the discerner of hearts. An example of this is the life of King David. Some of us might see his sin and come to the conclusion he didn't know God.

Perhaps, this is for you this morning, believer. You have fallen short. You have given in to some sinful behavior. You need help. You love Jesus but are weak. You have been judged for that behavior as one who does not know God. Let me encourage you. The God who fashioned your heart knows very well the inner workings. He alone understands why and how this particular sin has been so heavy on you. Please hear my heart. Don't stay there and feel trapped or victimized. Call on the name of Jesus for forgiveness today. Ask Him to set you free from this sin which holds you back from His wonderful plan for you. No matter what others say, if you are His, believe it and desire His Presence more than breath. He will meet you there.

Further Along the Way

Psalm 33:15 states, "the Lord looks out from His dwelling place and sees all the inhabitants of the earth." Does the fact that God can see everything at all times bring you comfort or does it cause you fear?

If you belong to Christ, this should bring you great hope and comfort. Why?

The verse ends with, "He who fashions the hearts understands their works." Look back at the text. What does the word *fashions* here mean? Do you see that the Lord was very careful and mindful as He put us together? Now consider how many times we, as believers, misjudge our brothers and sisters. Why do you think this is so? Could it be we have forgotten who created them? Do we forget there is a specific plan for their lives?

We have all sinned. Some sins are more obvious than others. However, all sin begins in the heart of man. Take time to enter into fellowship with the Lord today. Ask Him, the one who put your heart together, to uncover your sin. Pray for Him to cleanse and heal that area that causes you to be vulnerable to any specific sin.

Lastly, think of your brothers or sisters in Christ. Have you judged them? Take that to the Lord and ask Him to forgive you. Ask Him to do a work in that fellow believer's life. Trust the Lord with those you are concerned for and praise Him for moving in their lives.

Lord, help us to remember You know all Your children intimately. Rather than judge a brother or sister give us love so we may be moved to pray and help them.

Beggars

"When he saw Peter and John about to go into the temple, he began asking to receive alms." Acts 3:3

Here we see a beggar. If you go to the Scriptures in Chapter 3 of Acts, you will see an account of this beggar. He was crippled from his mother's womb. He would be laid at the temple gate daily to beg. Every day he would go through the same motions. I am sure he was well rehearsed in what he did and said.

I heard Jacki Pullinger, a missionary to Hong Kong, give a message on fasting once. She spoke about meeting beggars. She made this comment, and it always stuck with me: "Begging is hard work." She wasn't at all being funny or condescending. She pierced my heart with stories of the lengths people in poverty-stricken places had to go to beg or get people's attention. Some actually maimed themselves or their children to try to gain compassion. This was survival.

In the Scripture, this really stuck out to me. When the beggar saw Peter and John, he began to ask for alms. Doesn't seem too profound, I know. However, in my mind's eye, I see him. The beggar is going through the motions of the day. He sees them, and he does what he does every day, kind of like performing to get their attention. Begging has become natural for him. It's all in a day's work. I'm not being funny at all.

But this was not going to be an ordinary day for this beggar. The men were going to challenge him to hope for more than scraps this day. He was not going to get their pity, as he no doubt received from some. He was about to receive a new life.

The men demanded, "Look at us!" Then when he was giving them attention and expecting to receive, they gave him the hope of salvation. They proclaimed the name of Jesus to this man. They told him in so many words, "We do not have money for you, but we have something much more valuable and necessary—in the name of Jesus Christ the Nazarene, *walk*!"

This is just as powerful for us today. Sometimes we, too, go through the motions. We come to the gates of heaven, and we beg for this or that. But we are asking a miss. Peter and John said, "Look at us!" I believe the Lord is saying, "Look at Me!"

Gaze into the face of Jesus today. Receive something more valuable and necessary than what you have habitually been asking for. Be bold, repent and ask Him, "What have I been asking amiss? What must I pray and believe You for today? You occupy my thoughts. Help me to leave the beggarly things and ask the things of the Kingdom. I no longer want to be sitting outside. I want to be in Your very presence."

Further Along the Way

We sometimes have preconceived notions about those who beg. Can you think of some? Does my story of Jacki Pullinger and her message on begging change these notions?

The man at the gate begged daily. He most likely had a routine. In what way are we the same? Consider how we go through the same motions when we desire something from the Lord. In the apostles' ministry to this man, what did they demand him to do before he was healed? Do you think perhaps we are stuck in our situations because we fail to look up?

List some areas in your life where you need the Lord to move. In light of this devotional, would you agree we sometimes stay unhealthy because we are unwilling to move in closer and receive what the Lord has?

Father, I thank You that You are not satisfied to see us stay as we are. Bring us to a place where we will look up and see Your face and Your provision for us. Help us to realize You desire so much more for us than we ever ask.

No Where to call Home

"Then the scribe came and said to Him, 'Teacher, I will follow You wherever You go.' Jesus said to him, 'The foxes have holes and the birds of the air have nests, but the Son of Man has nowhere to lay His head.'" Matthew 8:19-20

Sailing from country to country can sound exciting to most people. It truly is an adventure. But when you are on a boat equipped to do missionary work, it's very different from cruise ships. It's small and congested, and it rocks all over as you sail. There are some breath-taking moments for sure; however, there are also some significant struggles. My struggle was battling horrendous migraines.

The verse above was brought to my memory during one of these battles. We had just sailed for several days. The altitude changes always triggered migraines. This particular day I was dreadfully ill. The pain in my head was overwhelming. It caused me to crawl to the bathroom countless times and hold my head over the toilet bowl. I was so weak. I lay there waiting for the doctor to come and give me an injection for pain. The injection was placed in my leg muscle and it really hurt, but it was worth the relief of the head pain. As I lay there waiting, I tried to get comfortable. Anyone who suffers migraines knows there is no position where your head is comfortable. I was feeling pretty pitiful and sorry for myself. I was thousands of miles from home, in pain, wanting to lay my head somewhere comfortable. But there was just nowhere to lay my head comfortably—and nowhere to call home.

While in tears, I heard a tender voice whisper in my spirit, *Foxes have holes and the birds have nests, but the Son of Man has nowhere to lay His head.* Instantly, my thoughts turned to Jesus. Now I was crying for Him. The profound truth hit me square between the eyes. Jesus left all the riches of the universe to come to earth where He didn't even have a place to call home. He traveled by foot. He rested wherever His Father's work took Him. His feet became blistered and painful. At times, He must have felt drained and parched. He was weak from His journey, and there was no place for Him to rest in his bed.

When Jesus was traveling one day, a scribe came to him. He blurted out, "Teacher, I will follow You wherever You go." What was Jesus' replay? "Foxes have holes and birds have nests, but I have nowhere to call home." Why such a sharp reply when this man was offering to follow Him? The Lord knows the heart of man. At times, man jumps quickly at the chance of perhaps an adventure. Man also desires to join those who have a following. At times, that pure excitement causes man to forget to consider the cost of what is being promised. He was making it clear to this man—following Him meant leaving the comforts of home, and very often it meant having no place to lay his head to rest. Instead of a soft pillow, there would be a rock. The man he desired to follow at this moment might be popular, but those praises would soon turn to jeers and hatred.

A few verses later, another man said to Jesus, "Lord, permit me first to go and bury my father." The Lord's reply to this man may seem even more severe—"Follow me and allow the dead to bury the dead."

This second man was already following the Savior, and yet, he requested to be excused for a season. It was the custom then for the son to care for his father until death. The father was still living. There was no way of knowing how long he would live. Jesus wasn't being cold and harsh; rather, He was making a point. If we are going to follow Him, we must be willing to go the long and rough road. There aren't breaks in discipleship. The call to be a disciple is moment by moment. We cannot lay it down and pick it up whenever there is a change in our lives. Our allegiance to the Lord goes above and beyond our family ties and traditions.

The point is the same today. There is a high cost to following Jesus. We have discipleship classes and read books on discipleship while in the comforts of home. Yet, do we really consider the cost of following Jesus closely. Jesus wants those who walk with Him and are intimate. He doesn't desire disciples who walk from a distance and are easily distracted by family and friends. There can be no agenda when following Christ other than to lay down our lives completely.

Further Along the Way

Like me, do you find yourself complaining at times that the place you are at is uncomfortable? You are following Jesus, but you just want a little break, just a place to lay your head and forget all the pain in life. How could the Lord's words in verses 19 and 20 of Matthew 8 bring you both conviction and encouragement?

We all have a certain amount of responsibility to care for our families. Jesus' reply to the disciple wanting to bury his father could seem harsh and insensitive. Do you now realize He was making a point? What point was He making? Do you believe, like a loving parent, He was cautioning for our own benefit? Why?

Many times in churches the cost of discipleship being presented pales in comparison to the joys of loving Jesus. What are perhaps the consequences of this? Do you feel people will leave fellowships if we tell them there is a cost? If so, what do you think Jesus' response would be, in light of all we discussed in the text above?

Take time to consider the cost of following Jesus. Ask the Lord to show you where you are failing to lay down your own agenda.

Father, help us to consider the great cost in following the Lord Jesus. He laid down His life in order to follow Your plan for salvation. Help us to lay down our lives to follow Him.

Blessed For Your Sake

"So it was, from the time that he had made him overseer of his house and all he had, that the Lord blessed the Egyptian's house for Joseph's sake; and the blessing of the Lord was on all that he had in the house and in the field." Genesis 39:5

Have you ever felt like you were in the wrong place? You begin your day asking, "What am I doing here?" Surely someone else can do better in this place than I, you reason. Sometimes you think you deserve better. You have been faithful. You have paid your dues. You feel discouraged, cheated, and down-right miserable.

Sometimes life seems so unfair, doesn't it? People around you are cheating their way through life, and it seems like they are being blessed for it. They have better jobs, better homes, a better marriage and more friends.

In Bible times and in recent years, believers have struggled through life, and as we look in the physical, it seems like they have little to show for it. Missionaries have spent years in foreign fields laboring for souls and have seen perhaps a handful really serve the Lord. Ministers here at home sometimes spend hours away from loved ones, as well. While they toil, digging up that hard ground, they are abused and gossiped about.

These thoughts were going through my mind as I was studying the life of Joseph. The above Scripture really hit me between the eyes the other day—"The Lord blessed the Egyptian's house for Joseph's sake." Joseph must have gone through times of discouragement. However, as we look at his life, he always had a sense of purpose. He knew in his heart of hearts that the Lord had a great plan. Everywhere he went, those around him were blessed. Whether he was a prisoner or a governor, the Lord caused people's lives to change around him.

Fellow servant of the Lord, be encouraged. As you go through your day, know that the Lord is causing ripples everywhere. Your presence alone is bringing the Light of eternity into other's lives. It's not because you are doing all the right things. Rather, it's because you are His, and He has a purpose. Wherever you find yourself today, that very place is being blessed for your sake. It might not seem so. I know. It seems like only chaos at times. I have wept many tears in my current place. But hold on to Him Who has called you. Be assured that the plan He has is much greater than you can imagine. His purposes are all for good. He plans to prosper you and give you hope right where you are.

Further Along the Way

Can you identify with the statement in the text, "What am I doing here?" Perhaps you wonder why others are enjoying success while you seem to be stuck. Could it be you fail to recognize God's purposes?

Do you believe God has a much bigger plan than what's visual or tangible?

Think back on the story of Joseph. How was he mistreated? Did life seem unfair?

God's hand was obviously on Joseph's life from the beginning. His plans were for good and to prosper Joseph. What if Joseph reacted in anger or bitterness, turning his heart from God? How do you believe his life would have turned out differently?

Think of how Joseph's life changes radically. Think of the place you are struggling now. Can you think of ways the Lord is blessing others just because you are there?

Are you able to see where He has already blessed you or others? An example would be when you were able to rise above difficulties, keeping a good attitude, even when others were unfair. You were a testimony of God's grace and love.

We often say, "God has a bigger purpose." What do you believe is His greatest purpose in every place He sends us as you consider eternity?

Father, how we desire to have a glimpse of the greater plan. Help us to be quiet before You and to listen to Your leading. Give us peace right where we are today.

Two Trees

"The serpent said to the woman, 'You surely will not die! For God knows that in the day you eat from it your eyes will be opened, and you will be like God, knowing good from evil.'" Genesis 3:4-5

As I was speaking with children the other morning about shepherds and sheep, the subject of adders (snakes) came up. One child, Daniel, hated snakes and was afraid of them and wouldn't even say the word snake. He asked, "Ms. Laurie, could you use another word please?" So, I said *serpent* when speaking about snakes.

I explained to this child that he is not alone; many are afraid of snakes. I shared that from the beginning of time snakes were seen as a curse or evil. Then I told him the story of Adam and Eve. I told the children there was a serpent in the garden God put them in. There were also trees, and one tree was off limits. They were not to touch or eat from this tree. It was the tree of the knowledge of good and evil. His interest was sparked. Children understand the concept of good and evil all too well today; their games are of power struggles between good and evil forces.

After hearing the story, this child understood why snakes have a bad reputation and better yet, why Adam and Eve were not to touch that tree. But I wonder how many believers understand? God was not withholding anything good from His children. His desires for His children have always been for their good. He did not want them to touch that tree because now they would have knowledge of not only good but evil. It was never the Lord's intention for us, the ones He loves so deeply, to know evil. He didn't want us to see evil, touch evil or have an understanding of how it works. The eating of the fruit of that tree was tragic! It broke the heart of the Father. He knew very well how this simple act would change everything. It would cause immeasurable pain and suffering, both to His children and to His Son.

We alone are like God in that we do have an understanding of good and evil. Let's keep that understanding under the instruction of the Holy Spirit, through His Word dwelling in us. In this way, we are set apart from all creation.

You may think your pet is wonderful and loving and all that but keep in mind, no other creation of the Lord is like Him in this manner. We are not like the animals, although some act as such. We are created in the image of the Almighty; therefore, we are accountable for our actions. Unfortunately, Adam and Eve did eat that fruit and now human nature is bent naturally toward evil. Yet, there is Hope.

There was another tree in another garden. It wasn't beautiful or tempting but it had more power than all the trees of the universe. Its power has less to do with its strength but all to do with its purpose. This tree held the prefect sacrifice. It held the One who redeemed all from the curse of sin. This tree had all that was good nailed upon it to crush all that was evil.

Come to this tree today. Come to the One Whose blood ran red that day and be cleansed from the evil that desires to take you. Remember, you are His. He desires only good for you, not evil.

Further Along the Way

Can you see how the original lie in the garden that God was holding back good from His children is still believable today? Do you sometimes feel the Lord is holding something back from you? Or that some of His "laws" are too strict?

Haven't you heard unbelievers stating the reason for not coming to Christ is it's no fun being a Christian, and there are too many rules? In light of what I have shared, what can you now tell them to dispel this lie?

Look back at the text. Why weren't Adam and Eve supposed to touch the tree? Do you see the protective side of God here, wanting to shield us from evil?

Scripture states that we are in the world but not of it. How do you think this point is made here? Do you think it's fair to say evil describes this world's system? Could this be what the Lord was protecting us from?

Think of some things you sense the Lord is telling you not to touch. Thank Him for His warnings and protection.

Father, thank You for always giving us warnings to stay clear of evil. Give us the grace to yield to those warnings. Thank You for the blood of Jesus shed on another tree for forgiveness when we do not heed Your warnings.

Straight from the Father

"Do not let your heart be troubled; believe in God, believe also in Me." John 14:1

This is such a familiar verse of Scripture. We hear it in songs and poetry about the Lord. Sometimes what is so common to us loses its severity. Jesus spoke these words to His disciples as He was explaining His leaving them. He goes on to tell them He goes to the Father. He says in His Father's house there are many rooms (dwelling places). It was during these last days with his disciples that He comforted them with these words—Let not your hearts be troubled. Although I am leaving, I am getting things ready for you to join Me in my Father's House.

This should bring us much comfort, shouldn't it? The world we live in is getting more and more hostile toward believers. Tolerance is being screamed for everything under the sun except for the ones who believe in the God of the Bible.

Thomas was concerned and troubled by Jesus' speaking of going away. He asked, "How do we get to where you are going?" Jesus said to him, "I am the way, the truth, and the life; no one comes to the Father but through Me." (John 14:6)

In a world that is rejecting absolutes more and more violently, here we read Jesus giving an absolute. There is only one way to the Father—Father God—and it is through Jesus Himself. How could Jesus dare to boast of being the *only* way? How could he be so intolerant of other's beliefs? Who does He think He is? Who do His followers think they are that they boast of knowing the *only* way?

The answer is simple and yet very profound. Jesus and the Father are one. There is no other way because Jesus Christ is the *only* One who actually came from the Father. He came from the bosom or heart of God Himself. He alone has the very essence of the Father. In human terms, He has the exact DNA. Please hear this. Only the Son of God came from the Father. Yes, we are children of God, and we are created by Him, but we are not as Jesus. He is the Father's very essence sent to us. Just as He returned to his Father and is seated with Him, we must also return to the Father. Jesus is the way and only way to get there.

Jesus was not being boastful when He spoke these words. He was loving His disciples and all who would come after them. He spoke these words out of great compassion. His desire is for you to come to the Father. He died for that desire to be realized. No one else could do this for us. It had to be Jesus.

Further Along the Way

Have you been asked why you believe Jesus is the only way to the Father? What has been your response? Does John 14:1 ("Believe in God, believe also in Me.") help you to answer? Why does this simple statement seem so hard for people to receive?

"Let not your hearts be troubled." In this world of many sorrows and tragedies, how can one take this instruction to heart? Jesus had previously told His disciples not to be troubled. He stated in this world there will be many tribulations, but He had overcome the world. What does this mean to you?

Have you experienced times when you could have been very troubled, yet you knew the peace and power of Christ instead? List those experiences. Give the Lord thanks for each one.

Soon we will all be with the Lord in His Father's house. Does this bring you comfort? Do you think the Lord would have you longing for this time? Can you experience this comfort here while on earth? Do you believe wherever you are can be His dwelling place? Are we to find His peace in all circumstances until His return?

Whatever is trying to trouble you today only has power over you if you allow it. Close in with the Lord and ask Him to refresh you today. Allow wherever you are today to be His dwelling place for you.

Father, help us today to understand Your words to us. Let it be a heart and spirit knowledge, not just a head knowledge. Thank You for loving us so deeply that You sent Your Only Son.

Oh, the Gall

"They tried to give Him wine mixed with myrrh; but He did not take it. It was the third hour when they crucified Him." Mark 15:23, 25

I have been very aware of the term *gall* lately, and its physical effects on the body. When the gallbladder, the organ which holds and filters fluid called bile or gall, isn't working properly, it feels like every time you eat, it turns to this bitterness in the belly which rises up to the throat causing nausea as it surfaces. It causes a nagging pain as well.

I've been pondering the term *gall* in the Scriptures recently as well. Gall is a mixture of very valuable, precious, costly herbs called myrrh and wine. This mixture is very bitter to taste or distasteful. As I was thinking on these things, the Lord, I believe, thought it good to give me an illustrative message recently.

I was at my nephew, Jordon's birthday party. It was held at the bowling alley in town. In walked a lady looking for someone. She stood there, and I noticed a very familiar face. It was an old friend from my college days. It had been close to thirty years since we saw each other. I said her name like a question. She looked over and mentioned my name as well. I was actually happy to see her and was about to engage in conversation. I had met her mother recently, and I mentioned that. This person totally blew me off. She looked right past me and walked away. Rude, rude, rude! I was embarrassed and offended at the same time. "Oh, the *gall* of her!" That's what went through my mind. I said to my sisters, who were sitting there when it happened, "I feel like going over to her and telling her what I think! How can someone be so rude?"

But, true to His character, Jesus whispered a certain "No." As I ponder all this, I am reminded this person was always pretty rude actually. When we were young and went out dancing together, I used to be embarrassed by how she treated others. She always had this way of acting as though she were better than everyone else. She, from my observation, hadn't really changed much through the years. Here's my point. When I was young, I may have felt embarrassed that she was rude, but we still hung out and had fun. But today, I would never choose to be friends with a person like this or spend time with her. It would not be much fun, being in the presence of a rude person.

Here's an even more important observation. Jesus would not allow me to "tell her off." In my heart I said, *Oh the gall of her,* meaning: How could she be so distasteful! But in reality, that same *gall* or *bitterness* was threatening to pollute my own heart at that moment. Oh sure, it would have felt good to tell her what I thought. The pain of feeling slighted would be numbed for a few minutes. However, I believe when we give into bitter, distasteful feelings, they will only ferment in our hearts and overflow. Here is where we choose between being *right* or righteous. I was right. She was indeed rude, but I needed to act as Jesus would—righteously.

While Jesus was being crucified, they tried to give Him gall on a sponge. It had some helpful priorities. The myrrh in the gall would have been a bit of a pain-reliever. It might have caused reactions in His body to quicken His death as well, thereby relieving His misery. However, Jesus chose to face the pain head on and to go through the pain we all deserved. Because He endured all the pain we deserved physically, we have healing now. Jesus is the Balm of Gilead. He is in a real sense our Myrrh, our healing ointment.

Today, as people rub you the wrong way, take the Name of Jesus with you. Apply that Name, that healing balm to whatever ails you. Are you feeling rejected, slighted, heart-broken, depressed, anxious, physically unhealthy or faint? The bride in Song of Solomon says of the Bridegroom, "My lover is like a bundle of myrrh between my breasts." How fitting for all of us today. We are His bride and as we pull this bundle of myrrh, Jesus, close to us, holding Him between our breasts where the heart lies, He will heal all those issues which flow from the heart.

Further Along the Way

In my above account, I wanted to tell this lady what I thought. You too may have had a similar experience. Considering the nature of the person, what might her reaction have been? Do you think I would be in any way demonstrating Christ's ways if I went ahead with my emotions?

At the cross, Jesus was clearly in agony. He could have demanded angels to come and free Him, but He chose to stay. Gall was a temporary pain-reliever and may have taken the edge off. Why did He go as far as to refuse the smallest amount of relief? Consider your answer. Does this make you feel like you can be victorious over bitterness and other sins? Why?

It's painful to remember being hurt or rejected by another, especially a friend. But for the sake of healing, name someone out loud that hurt you. Ask the Lord to search your heart and see if there is bitterness or gall fermenting there. Ask Jesus to cleanse and heal that wounded area of your heart. Speak his or her name out loud again, this time asking the Lord to forgive them for their sin against you.

Spend time praising the Lord for taking that bitter cup so that you would not have to hold on to bitterness.

Father, thank You for sending us Your Son as a perfect example of the manifestation of Your righteousness. He could have fought to be freed from the agony. But for our sake, He chose the pain rather than relief. Help us to live as Christ.

He Moves In Great Mercy

"But God who is rich in mercy, because of His great love with which He loved us, even when we were dead in trespasses, made us alive together with Christ (by grace you have been saved)."
Ephesians 2:4-5

"Three little monkeys jumping on a bed...." Remember that nursery rhyme? I do. I used to teach it to toddlers. The children would laugh and giggle. I imagine they had visions of cute, little, smiling monkeys jumping and having fun. American children can afford to see monkeys this way because they usually see them from a distance. However, their African counterparts wouldn't see them the same way.

African monkeys might be seen running for their lives rather than jumping on a bed. I know of at least one such monkey. Jeaneth, Maria and I were about to get into the car. I would often give these girls a ride to school. As I opened the car door, I could hear a loud screeching noise. It got higher and higher and fiercer and fiercer. We looked up in the tree and there he was—a monkey. What was he screeching at? Men. Men were everywhere. They were climbing up the tree with machetes. Tree bark was flying all over.

I asked the girls, "What are they all doing to that poor monkey?" Their reply angered me, "They are getting the monkey for the Songoma (witchdoctor). She will kill it and use it for Muti (medicine)." I was furious! I did what any good missionary would. I yelled, "Get down from that tree!" When there was no response, I yelled even louder, "I hope that monkey bites you!"

Poor Jeaneth and Maria. They are Sotho speaking and knew they had to translate my words of wisdom. When the translation was done, the men looked at me in dismay. The monkey got away, and the men came down from the tree. I could see a trail of tree bark as we drove to the girl's school.

As we continued on our way, I asked the girls questions. I knew a bit about the practice of sacrificing monkeys for the witchdoctor's divination. Like so many African practices, it was beyond my understanding. So I questioned and commented. I commented on the evils of selling monkeys, of blood sacrifices, and such. They politely listened.

Jesus was also listening. We think we are so smart at times, but he knows better. What was I so concerned about? Our tree? African trees are very beautiful, but I wasn't concerned for the tree. The monkey? All who know me well know I am no animal activist. In fact, most animal activists confuse me. They seem to

114

care more for animals than people. So, what was bothering me so much?

Jesus is the discerner of hearts, and He knows His children so well. He spoke the answer to my heart—*principle*. The fact that these men were going to sell the monkey to a witchdoctor really boiled me! That was evil. Wasn't I justified in my anger? After all, it was righteous anger, right? Sounds pretty convincing. However, not to Jesus. His thoughts are so much higher than ours. Where we move in righteous anger, He moves in mercy. Where we see principle, He extends love. Love for whom? No, not so much for the monkey. Although He created the little fellow, He loves man so much more. Remember, man is created in His very image.

Jesus posed this question to my spirit, "Why weren't you concerned with those men? They are the ones in risk of death—spiritual death. Did it occur to me that for them to go to such lengths to get that monkey, they were indeed in great bondage?"

Are we so sold on principle that we don't see the condition of another man's heart and even more importantly, his soul?

What principle do you stand for? Is it the way people dress in church? Are you so concerned with their clothes that you don't get close enough to see their heart? Maybe it's the way people act that concerns you. They are too loud, or they are too timid. They speak rudely to you. They ignore you, so you write them off. You think to yourself that if they were *real* Christians they would know how to act, and you miss an opportunity to minister.

There are so many examples where Jesus was merciful while man stood on principle. The pages of the Bible are full of such examples: the man healed on the Sabbath, the lady caught in adultery, and the woman with the alabaster jar just to name a few.

Yes, we have a Savior who will always move in the way of grace and always in the way of mercy. As I write this, I am reminded of another sacrifice on another tree. The men watching yelled, "If you are the Son of God, come down from that cross." But His mercy said, *no.* Principle said, "The penalty for sin is death." And that is absolute justice. Mercy said, "I know. I will die for them."

Further Along the Way

Having principles and values are good things. From the story, how can they get in our way?

Can you think of times when you may have held tightly to a certain principle and missed an opportunity to minister?

John 3:16 is a well-known Scripture. It is perhaps one of the most quoted by believers. Look this Scripture up if you are unfamiliar with it. What does the verse state as the cause for God giving His own Son for us? According to this, what is much more important to the Lord than principles?

How does the fact that God loves us enough to give His Son bring you assurance? Can you better understand how much He values a relationship with us?

Father, we often miss it when it comes to the greatness of Your love and mercy. Help us to grow deeper in our understanding so we can be made perfect in Your love. May our desire be to demonstrate that love and mercy to others.

Bottled Tears

"You have taken account of my wanderings; Put my tears in Your bottle. Are they not in Your book?" Psalm 56: 8

Here we see David on the run from his enemies, and he is crying out to the Lord for help. I love studying the life of King David because he is so real and so human. No superhero here. He makes many blunders and humbly admits them all.

In this passage he tells the Lord, "You have taken account of my wanderings." He is stating to the Lord that he knows although he has been on the run again for his life, he is very aware that the Lord is there for him. David had many who loved him, but he also had many who hated him. This time their warfare used was in the way of twisting all David had said and trying to make him as an evil liar. These enemies were the original "haters" in a true sense of that word. Today, we call those who do not agree with our lifestyles or opinions "haters," but the haters here were ready to kill David. Do you realize to hate someone in the biblical sense of the word actually means to want to harm or even kill them? In a real sense, we can "kill" a person with our words; we kill their reputation and damage their spirit.

Perhaps some of us can identify with David. We have been serving the Lord. We aren't perfect, and we plead for the mercy of the Lord. There are others who have taken what we meant for good or to bless others, and they have twisted the truth and caused others to act in a hateful manner toward us or caused damage to our reputations. Be encouraged, we are no different than David in the Lord's eyes. He has taken account of our every wandering.

He has put our tears in His bottle. This is so powerful to me. It should also be to you, my friends in Christ Jesus. The God of the universe has seen your wanderings, and He has witnessed all the tears you have shed. He has been mindful of them and has saved them. Elsewhere in Scripture it is stated that God is intimate with our ways. He is so close to those who fear Him and love His Name—like a loving husband who has been with his wife through many experiences and notices a change in countenance. Because he is so intimate with her, He sees her pain and the tears forming before they are shed. That's how our loving God is.

"Are they not in Your book?" What book? If you look in Malachi 3:16, you see that all our wanderings, all our inner thoughts , all our love and concerns are recorded in the Lord's book of remembrance. The Lord of all creation has your name written in His Book and your tears in a bottle. You and I are so blessed and so loved.

Further Along the Way

People sometimes misunderstand our words or actions. Worse yet, they accuse us of being a liar or evil. Has this happened to you? How did you react? What were you feeling?

The Scripture above states the Lord knows all our wanderings. We can conclude by this that nothing escapes the Lord's knowing the truth. In light of this, can you see where asking the Lord to vindicate you is the best course of action when being wrongly accused?

Think of a situation in your life where you felt like you shed enough tears to fill a bottle. Does it bring you comfort knowing He kept those seemingly wasted tears and saved them in a bottle?

Today, consider those you come in contact with. Ask the Lord to give you His heart for them, asking that He would show you the truth in all matters. If the Lord brings a need for forgiveness to your spirit, go and forgive. Also ask forgiveness for times you misunderstood and falsely accused someone else.

Psalm 56:8 states, "You have taken account of my wanderings; put my tears in a bottle." Let's take time to consider this truth.

Sometimes it's our wanderings which cause our tears. Do you see places you've wandered which caused heartache? Have you wandered from God? Even though you may have wandered, isn't it wonderful to know He has never lost sight of you?

Father, help us to have a heart like Yours. When people are mocking, threatening and speaking all kinds of evil, help us to pray, "Forgive them. They know not what they do."

Bruised Reeds

"A bruised reed He will not break, and smoking flax He will not quench, till He sends forth justice to victory." Matthew 12:20

I have the joy of caring for a woman who the Lord has blessed with ninety-six years. As part of our morning ritual, I bathe her. I am careful to be gentle, and she often jokes that I touch her like a "momma with her baby." As careful as I am though, at times she will flinch and say, "There's a tender spot." A closer look shows she has a bruise under her skin. She has golden, brown skin so the bruise isn't obvious at first, but now that I've seen it, I must be more careful. As her caregiver, I am to do all that is possible to not add to her bruising. Further, I hope to be able to restore her skin completely.

My experience with this precious lady makes me think of a bigger picture of us as the church. We are surrounded daily with people who have hidden bruises. The Lord has sent us to be a safe place for them to expose their wounds. Once we realize they have been bruised in a certain area, we as God's caregivers are to be careful in the way we touch their lives. With our actions and words we are to be sure there isn't further bruising. Like myself with this precious lady, we are to take all measures possible to restore that person.

Jesus is the Redeemer. By definition, a redeemer restores that which he has created. Jesus not only heals but brings them back to pristine condition. Furthermore, He desires to bring that bruised person to a place of treasure that they would never had imagined or dreamed of. He has called us to be His caregivers. Once those precious ones feel free enough to expose their wounds, Jesus desires to restore them through our love and care.

What a blessed privilege God has set before us. And yet the challenge can seem overwhelming at times. People who have been the most bruised often act unlovable. "Hurting people hurt people." We have all heard that saying, and there is some truth in that. I have a counter saying for that, "Healed people heal people." We as messengers of Christ can love freely because He has shed His love in our hearts by His Holy Spirit. Remember, He was already bruised for the bruised.

When the challenge seems great, try to reflect on the times He has healed your wounds. Look at your scars and remember His. Understand that scars don't hurt anymore but open wounds do. So, look at the places from which He has already healed you and share from those experiences. I believe as you do those open wounds of yours will become healed and become scars to further heal from. It really is a win-win situation.

Further Along the Way

In the first paragraph of the story, the lady says, "There's a tender spot." Do you believe there are tender spots in our lives? If so, how do you react when that tender spot is rubbed the wrong way?

Let's consider that if we have tender spots, those who come in contact with us do also. As believers, what is our responsibility when someone reveals a bruise or tender spot? How did Jesus treat those who were hurting? Matthew 12:20 answers this.

Do you remember times when you were hurting and, therefore, hurt others? What, if any, was a source of healing for you? I believe healed people heal people. Do you agree? If so, consider how you can move from hurting to healing.

List some areas in life where you have been healed. Now pray and ask the Lord to lead you to people where you can demonstrate his healing power.

Father, thank You for sending Your only Son to redeem the lost and hurting. Help us to remember Your desire is never to crush but to restore. Thank You for my many scars for they remind me of Your work in my life.

Higher Ground

"The end of all things is near; therefore, be of sound judgment and sober spirit for the purpose of prayer. Above all, keep fervent in your love for one another, because love covers a multitude of sins." 1 Peter 4:7-8

The above Scriptures have been in my heart, mind and spirit for days now. Seems whenever I have a quiet time with the Lord, I am brought to being of sound judgment and sober spirit for the sake of prayer, loving one another. Sometimes the Scripture which has come to me has been even stronger—mourn and weep, bow your head.

Read the above verses once again. Do you see why the two verses fit so well together? Prayer, my friend, is the key to all things which are pleasing to the Lord. God does not want us to mourn, weep or be sober in spirit for the sake of being morbid. Not at all. I sense He is calling all believers to be quiet before Him for the time is short, and there is an urgency being felt on the earth. Be sober in spirit. My former pastor used to preach, "The church wants to swing from the chandeliers, but it's a time to be on our faces weeping." There is absolutely a time to dance and rejoice, but there is also a time to be quiet, enter in and intercede for one another. How can we, as believers, discern anything when we are being so loud and distracted?

Be quiet for the sake of prayer. Love one another fervently. Let's ask ourselves if we are being fervent in our love for one another. If we have bad feelings and are harboring un-forgiveness in our hearts toward each other, how can we be loving? If you are at a loss of how to forgive your brother or sister in Christ, the answer is in the verses above. Pray for them. In praying for that person, you will be blessing them. When you bless someone in prayer, you are mentioning them to the Father and speaking all good things. Your heart will melt and change into the Lord's love for that person. If that person has sinned against you that love will cover all the sins committed.

Pray, pray, pray and allow the Holy Spirit to consume all that is hurtful in your heart. You, my brother and sister, be clean of un-forgiveness today. Time really is short. Leave all that petty stuff at the cross. We must be about our Father's business. The Holy Spirit is calling us to higher ground. It's time to move up.

Further Along the Way

The above Scripture states the end of all things is near. Yet this was written over two thousand years ago. What is happening globally which confirms this statement for today? With the end times approaching even closer today, why is it so essential for us to be people of prayer?

"The church wants to swing from the chandeliers, but it's a time to be on our faces." Why do you think believers are consumed with having fun in the church? Do you think it may be because we do not want to face the hurt in our lives and the lives of others? Consider the condition of the world. How could this be dangerous?

The verses also admonish us to love one another fervently. Why is the Scripture pointing to our relationship to each other in the body rather than our relationship to non-believers? Do you believe our love for one another somehow directly impacts those outside the church?

Why do you think it's so difficult to forgive? According to the text, how are we to forgive each other?

What are the benefits of praying for someone? For ourselves? Consider at least one person who has wronged you. Seek the Lord, and ask for Him to search your heart. Is there un-forgiveness? Pray for grace to forgive. Pray for the Lord to bless this other person.

How can someone be sure they are praying the heart of God? Ask the Lord to show you the dead things in your prayer list. Allow Him to give you peace with those petty things, so you can move on to what's most important.

Father, help us to walk close enough to You that our hearts are being cleansed daily. Lord, we rejoice for what Your Son Jesus has already done in us. Teach us through Your Holy Spirit how to discern the times. You give us seasons to rejoice as well as to weep in step with Your Spirit.

Forsaken?

"At the ninth hour Jesus cried out with a loud voice, 'Eloi, Eloi, Lama Sabachthani?'['My God, My God, why have You forsaken Me?']" Mark 15:34

I was having lunch with good friends recently and this Scripture came up. The question was raised about how to explain this Scripture. Had God the Father, Who loved His Son Jesus immeasurably, actually forsaken Him at His greatest hour of need?

Many of us know this is what Jesus cried out loudly from the cross. Some realize this very Scripture He cried out was quoting the words of David in Psalm 22. I encourage you to read this psalm today and be amazed at what David spoke thousands of years before Christ's crucifixion. Hearing Jesus quote from this psalm surely would have pierced the hearts of some of the Jews standing there before the cross. They would have known this verse well. But still for us, the question of being forsaken remains.

After our lunch, the Lord brought back a memory to me. This may help us understand better. I share this with great reverence because God's ways are so much higher than ours and none of us can understand the depths of what He is saying to us. I only share to shed a bit of light and hopefully encourage you.

As most of you know my niece, Ella Rose, had a bone marrow transplant at fifteen months. It was a heart wrenching time. One memory always stands out to me. I went to Boston Children's Hospital and visited my little Peanut. She was in isolation and nothing could touch this child unless it was purified first. We were all very careful. My sister, Annmarie, was standing in front of the huge crib the baby was in. The baby stood there peering over the side trying to hug her Mommy. She kept grabbing for Mommy's face and wanted to kiss her on the mouth. This was very normal for Ella, but her mom had to turn her face away every time. It was heart breaking to watch, but it was for Ella Rose's good.

God was doing an amazing work and certain things had to be done for that work to be complete. He is all loving and powerful and could have spoken a word and Ella Rose would have been healed on the spot, but in His great wisdom and way, which we cannot always comprehend, Ella Rose went through shear torment the following months. After all the chemo, she became violently ill and gained ten pounds of water weight. She was in horrible pain. The hardest part for me was knowing the child lay there in pain crying out for Mommy, but by this point, to touch the baby would cause more pain. I remember my sister asking for prayer, "I just want to be able to hold my baby again." I remember a family member sharing upon her visit to the ICU Ella that Rose was so weak all she could say in a faint voice was, "Ma. Ma."

If it seems insensitive to share my niece's experience to shed light on Jesus' crying out to His Father, please forgive me. I never take the severity of God's Word lightly. Here's what I feel the Lord put in my spirit. Jesus was God's beloved Son. There will never be a relationship comparable to the love the Father and Son share. They have been together from the beginning of time. Their relationship, like no other, is eternal in length. Their love is beyond measure.

When Jesus cried out to His Father, He was torn, literally. At this point, He was unrecognizable to even His family and followers. He was a mangled piece of flesh by now. His emotions were raw as He was raw from head to toe. I am not trying to offend, but you need to grasp the severity. He's asking the Father, "Why have You forsaken Me?" Remember, Jesus came in humanity at this point. He hadn't forgotten His purpose in going to the cross. This was Him asking, "Why couldn't You rescue Me? Why couldn't there be a better way?" Similar to His cry in the garden, "If it be Your will, take this cup from Me."

Did the Father forsake Him? Absolutely not. But He had to move beyond the horrendous pain for the sake of *all* mankind. This was the only way to salvation. Jesus had to go through the suffering for the healing of all nations to come just as my sister had to turn away and not pick up her crying baby. She knew new life would come out of this pain.

I humbly pray this sheds some light. Again, I am not trying to lighten the severity of what happened. I am seeing this with a human heart. Believer, we should be so very thankful for what Jesus went through. He didn't get down from that cross or refuse to carry it. He felt forsaken in a very dark and heart-wrenching time.

He knows our pain, as well. He knows how we feel when we are rejected because His own people rejected Him. He understands when we feel abandoned—His followers all scattered. He identifies with us when we feel helpless and alone—He watched His mother at the foot of the cross feeling pain and helplessness. Finally, He has experienced a time of darkness— there was no darker time in history then when He had every sin ever committed put on Him.

The greatest work was done through the blood of the Lamb. There was no other way for us to come to the Father. This should cause us to shout loudly, "Worthy is the Lamb Who was slain from the foundations of the earth!"

Go on your way today knowing Jesus has experienced all you will be concerned about. His last words were, "Father, into Your hands I commit My Spirit." Let us all do the same. Blessings.

Further Along the Way

Did you realize the shout from the cross in the above Scripture was referring to Psalm 22? If you haven't spent time in this psalm, please do so. This was all Jesus would willingly endure. It will shed light on many areas of His suffering.

Have you ever questioned the words spoken on the cross? If you are troubled by the thought of the Father seemingly forsaking His Son, keep in mind all the Father does is in view of eternity. Every action He takes is drenched in justice and love.

Knowing the Lord would not withhold the life and suffering of His own Son for our sakes should be a cause of great gratitude. How do you think you could demonstrate gratitude better?

Can you identify with my sister's pain as a parent wanting to comfort her child and being prevented for the greater good? How does this cause you to see the heart of Father God during His Son's suffering?

Take time to focus on all the things Jesus walked through while here on earth that mirrored our own trials. Look back over the text and consider how He was rejected, abandoned, insulted, abused, and how He felt all alone and helpless. How does this help you feel freer to come to Him for comfort when going through trials?

Use the above mentioned Scripture as a spring board to praise and give Him thanks.

Do you see now why all of heaven says, "Worthy is the Lamb who was slain"?

Father, thank You a million times over for Your great sacrifice. I will never completely realize Your pain in giving Your son. I ask that You give me glimpses of Your love as I study Your Word.

Little Rocks

"My soul waits in silence for God only; from Him is my salvation. He only is my rock and my salvation, my stronghold; I shall not be greatly shaken." Psalm 62:1-2

My soul waits in silence for God only—isn't this a tall order for most of us? Waiting without pleading and begging. Waiting without speaking. Silence. I think this generation especially struggles with the issue of silence. We are so overly stimulated with media. Even our places of worship, where we are supposed to enter in and hear Him, are full of stimulation. It's a wonder anyone ever hears His still, small voice.

Nonetheless, the psalmist says he is silent before the Lord. He goes on to state that the Lord is his salvation and his rock—His *only* salvation and rock.

Here's where we are challenged. We find it difficult to walk in the truth stated above. The Lord is our *only* way of salvation. We, as believers, all agree He is our only way to eternity, but salvation has a wider scope than just our eternal life. Is He also the One we trust to save us from all aspects of our lives with things like financial ruin, persecution, illness, or pain of broken relationships? I don't say He will spare us from these, but only *He* will steady us through them.

We have all had times when we were shaken to our cores. I remember in a very literal sense being shaken the morning of my cancer surgery. Ironically, the anti-anxiety medication was causing me to tremble all over. In addition to the physical shaking were the waves of emotions trying to chisel away at my belief in a solid rock foundation. During this time my sister, Teresa, was with me every moment. I always call her my "little rock" because she is so balanced. She is steady in her love and devotion to me. I can count on her.

As much as we all might have "little rocks" in our lives, those we lean on and trust more than others can only bring us so far. They are just like us. They are limited in their ability to make it all better. I tease Teresa about being my "little rock." I always remind her that Jesus is my *Big Rock*. He is the One I still myself before when the world is shaking around me. He is unmovable— my stronghold. Even though He steadies me in all the issues of life, He doesn't always rescue me. I have to walk through many storms, but He keeps me going forward.

He is the same for you, my fellow believer. He is your *Rock*. He is your *only* salvation. He has not only saved you from eternal damnation, but He desires to get you through all the storms of life, such as finances, health, pain of broken relationships, and persecutions. He asks one thing of you. Be silent and still before Him. Trust Him to be your Big Rock. Be thankful for the "little rocks" He has placed in your life, while realizing they are given so you will see glimpses of His care for you.

Further Along the Way

In Psalm 62, the psalmist begins by stating he is waiting in silence. Why do you think it is important to be quiet? Do you sometimes have difficulty being silent or finding a place of quiet? Consider what you can change in the way of time or place so you can be silent.

I shared how my sister, Teresa, is my "little rock." Who is your little rock? Even though others are a great comfort to us, why is it necessary to keep in mind they are just like us and, therefore, limited?

Why do I say Jesus is my "Big Rock"? Look back at Psalm 62 and focus on verse 2. How is the Lord defined as a "Rock" according to this verse? When you consider all the personal trials you face and all the turmoil in the world, how is knowing this a comfort to you?

Make a list of times He has steadied you in the times of issues with finances, illness, pain of broken relationships and persecution. Give thanks for all those times. How does this build your faith in the "Big Rock," Jesus?

Father, thank You for being our "Big Rock." Help us to remember even though You have given us little rocks, You are our constant and consistent help in times of trouble.

After Words

I am so blessed you have walked this journey of soul piercing with me. I pray you realize how very loved you are by the One Who formed you. Never lose sight of what Jesus Christ has done for you at the cross. Let this truth be your foundation. I pray these devotionals have helped you to understand the value He has placed on your life.

His Word is powerful and life changing. I have stood on His promises for thirty years now and have never been disappointed. The road has often been rough, but He has steadied my feet all the way and has pierced through my darkest times with His light. I will never be the same. I pray the same for you, the reader. Be a lover of His Word and His presence and watch Him work in ways you have never imagined.

Until our next journey together—or until Jesus calls us home. Be blessed and take the precious name of Jesus with you.

Made in the USA
Charleston, SC
21 December 2015